575

# Current
# Auditing Developments

# Current Auditing Developments

## Third Edition

Compiled and Edited by
EMILE WOOLF, FCA, FCCA, FBIM

**Published by Van Nostrand Reinhold (UK) Co. Ltd.**
**Molly Millars Lane, Wokingham, Berkshire, England**

Printed in Great Britain at the
University Press, Cambridge

# Preface to the Third Edition

Recent examination papers in Auditing clearly indicate the extent to which examiners expect candidates studying this subject at an advanced level to have kept abreast with contemporary developments. Of all fees earned in most professional practices the largest proportion is attributable to auditing work and, unlike years gone by, developments today tend to take place at a pace which at times is bewildering.

No textbook, viewed from this point of view, can provide all the information required, and students are therefore constantly entreated by their tutors to make full use of the professional press in order to obtain a grasp of the latest legislation; new developments in case law; the implications for auditors of new Accounting Standards; recommendations of the Consultative Committee of Accountancy Bodies (CCAB); the pronouncements of the Auditing Practices Committee (APC); especially the new Auditing Standards and the host of related Guidelines; reports of Department of Trade Inspectors; as well as developments at the international level which have a powerful influence on UK practice.

Following the publication in 1980 of the first definitive UK Auditing Standards, the APC has embarked upon an extensive programme of updating earlier professional recommendations and reissuing them in the form of Guidelines, always referencing their content to the full Standards by which all UK auditors are now bound. Although it would be tempting to include all of them in this text in full, such a policy would leave little room for other material. Those which simply update or replace extant material, rather than breaking new ground, have therefore been omitted. Students are nevertheless entreated to be alert to the issue of new Guidelines by subscribing to those accountancy journals which always reproduce them immediately following publication.

The purpose of this publication, which is updated regularly whenever the need arises, is to bring together a compilation of all such developments which have take place during the two years or so prior to publication, retaining those chapters that have continuing relevance. It is not all work of original authorship, and I am indebted to the Bodies who have provided much of the source material which is included, particularly to the APC for their permission to reproduce certain passages from their invaluable quarterly bulletin, *True & Fair*. I would like to give special acknowledgement to the usefulness of the Accounting & Auditing Newsletter produced internally by Deloitte, Haskins & Sells, from which certain passages (notably on the problems of deferred taxation) have been taken.

Wider reading is obviously advisable at all times; nonetheless, students will find that this volume represents a useful point of reference on all matters of contemporary concern to the UK auditing profession and is, as such, an invaluable source of examination material. It should be remembered that many examination papers are set as far as 9 months ahead of the actural date of sitting. A number of chapters in this text are based upon my own *Manual of Auditing*.

Certain recent examinations have already included questions on subject matter dealt with herein; students should always bear in mind that important topics bear frequent repetition in examination papers — especially where the general standard of answers at prior sittings has been felt by the examiners to be disappointing.

In this edition the whole text has been updated and I have incorporated new material on the Companies Act 1981; auditors' independence; new case law on liability to third parties; the audit implications of the latest Accounting Standards and exposure drafts; small company audit problems; new Guidelines on post-balance sheet events, management representations, and prior period comparatives; the risk-based audit approach; and additional notes on the impact on auditing of mini-computers and remote terminals. It is my hope and belief that this new edition will prove to be an ideal reference medium for those preparing for auditing examinations, and who therefore require an authoritative compendium of recent developments.

*Emile Woolf*

# Contents

# 1 The Auditor and the Companies Acts

*UK company law is spread over five statutes at the present time. The principal Act remains the Companies Act 1948, and the Acts of 1967, 1976, 1980 and 1981, respectively, may be thought of as legislation which partly amends and partly extends that embodied in the principal Act. The ensuing pages have been set out to provide auditing students with a detailed summary of all companies' legislation which has a direct effect on auditors acting in a statutory capacity.*

## Appointment (Section 14, 1976)

Basic Rule: *Every* company shall at *each* AGM appoint an auditor (or auditors) to hold office until the conclusion of the next AGM.
  Exceptions:

  (a) The directors may appoint:
      (i)   the first auditors, to hold office until the conclusion of the first AGM,
      (ii)  auditors to fill a casual vacancy.
  (b) The Secretary of State may appoint auditors if neither members nor directors have done so. The company has a duty to inform the Secretary within one week of this power becoming exercisable.

*Note:*  Under pre-1976 legislation it was possible for retiring auditors to be automatically reappointed without any resolution being passed.

## Removal (Sections 14 & 15, 1976)

A company may by ordinary resolution remove an auditor before the expiry of his term of office. Where such a resolution is passed the company shall notify the Registrar of Companies within 14 days.

*Note 1:*  resolutions at a general meeting for which *special notice* (28 days) is required:

  (a) appointing an auditor *other* than the retiring auditor;
  (b) filling a casual vacancy;
  (c) reappointing a retiring auditor originally appointed by directors to fill a casual vacancy;
  (d) removing an auditor before expiry of term of office.

*Note 2:*  steps designed to protect the retiring auditor from unwarranted dismissal:

  (a) On receipt of such notice the company shall send a copy to the existing auditor.
  (b) The auditor has the right to make representations in writing, not exceeding a reasonable length, and may request that these shall be notified to the members.
  (c) Upon receipt of such representations the company has a duty:
      (i)   in any notice of resolution given to members of the company, to state the fact of the representations having been made; and
      (ii)  to circularise copies of the representations to every person entitled to receive notice of the meeting.
  (d) If the representations are not circularised as prescribed (either because received too late or

due to the company's default) the auditor may have them read out at the meeting, quite apart from his right to be heard orally on any matter which affects him as auditor.

(e) The representations need not be circularised, nor will the auditor possess the right to have them read out the meeting if, on the application of any person who claims to be aggrieved by the contents thereof, the court is satisfied that the auditor is abusing his rights in order to secure needless publicity for defamatory matter. The court may order the costs of such an application to be borne (wholly or in part) by the auditor.

## Rights of Ex-auditor (Section 15, 1976)

An auditor who has been *removed* may

(a) attend the general meeting at which his term of office *would* have expired, and
(b) attend any general meeting at which it is proposed to fill the vacancy caused by his removal, and
(c) be heard at any such meeting on any business which concerns him as former auditor.

## Remuneration (Section 14, 1976)

The auditor's remuneration shall be fixed by whoever makes the appointment. In practice this is not necessarily fixed in advance, the auditor simply making clear (in the letter of engagement) the basis of arriving at the audit fee. The audit fee, together with the expenses incurred in connection with the audit, must be disclosed in the company's published accounts regardless of how the fees are determined. It is usual practice for every AGM agenda to include an item which authorises the directors to fix the auditor's remuneration, thereby avoiding the need for it to approved in advance by the members, and at the same time enabling auditors to bill for their work on an interim basis.

## Qualification (Section 161, 1948; and Section 13, 1976)

The following are *not* qualified to act as auditor of a limited company:

(a) a body corporate;
(b) a person who is not a member of one of the following:
   The Institute of Chartered Accountants in England and Wales
   The Institute of Chartered Accountants of Scotland
   The Institute of Chartered Accountants in Ireland
   The Association of Certified Accountants
(c) an officer or servant of the company;
(d) a partner or employee of an officer or servant of the company.

*Explanatory notes regarding the above*

*(a) Body Corporate:* a legal 'person', the liability of whose members is usually limited in some way. The audit is in the nature of a personal service, and this is incompatible with the idea of limited liability. The auditor is to be regarded as personally responsible for the quality of his work and that of any persons to whom he may delegate it.

It is of interest to note, however, that professional bodies in the USA and UK are currently seeking to obtain some form of limited liability, especially due to the increased range of potential liability that has become apparent in recent years, and the difficulty in obtaining adequate insurance cover for professional negligence risks. It is suggested that liability should be restricted in proportion to the audit fee (e.g. ten times the fee), with a specified maximum upper limit. Presumably, the 'price' of such a limitation would be:

(i) a suitable form of disclosure of the firm's accounts; and
(ii) a requirement to guarantee professional indemnity insurance cover up to the amount of maximum liability.

At the time of writing, however, no definitive proposals have been published.

*(b) Professional qualification.* (i) Apart from what is specified above, the Secretary of State will grant similar status to the holder of an equivalent qualification obtained abroad, provided reciprocal arrangements exist in the country concerned for holders of UK qualifications. This is of special relevance to those UK auditors wishing to practice in the USA, Canada and the EEC countries.

(ii) Any person without a professional qualification, but holding Department of Trade authority as having had equivalent experience in practice prior to 6 August 1947 (the date the 1948 Act was introduced as a Bill), *may accept appointment without restriction.*

(iii) Any person without a professional qualification, but who has had sufficient experience as an accountant and auditor in practice throughout the 12 months to 3 November 1966 and was on that date the duly appointed auditor of at least one company classed as an 'exempt private company', may continue to act as auditor of limited company clients and may accept further such appointments, *provided* that no shares or debentures of the company in question have been quoted publicly.

*(c) Officer or servant.* Any member of staff on the full-time payroll establishment may be regarded as a servant for this purpose. 'Officer' is defined in Section 455 (1948) — the 'definitions' section — as including a director, secretary or manager.

*(d) Partner or Employee of officer or servant.* If, for example, A, B and C are partners in the firm of ABC & Co., chartered or certified accountants, and A is also a director of XYZ Ltd.:

(i) he obviously cannot act as auditor of XYZ Ltd., since he is an officer;
(ii) neither B nor C can act as auditors of XYZ Ltd., since they are *partners* of an officer (A) of the company. Similarly, the firm ABC & Co. cannot be appointed auditors;
(iii) the managing clerk, L, of ABC & Co. cannot act as auditor of XYZ Ltd., even though he may have the necessary professional qualifications, since he is an *employee* of an officer (A) of the company.

*But note:* that if L were a director of a family company LMN Ltd., there would be no legal objection (except in the unlikely event of LMN Ltd. being a building society — Building Societies Act 1962) to ABC & Co. acting as auditors of LMN Ltd., since A, B and C would be *employers* of an officer of the company. From the independence point of view this is clearly undesirable but there is no legal objection.

## Status

The question of the auditor's precise status has been raised from time to time. It is fairly safe to regard him as agent for the members to whom he is responsible *(Spackman v. Evans)*. In this 19th century House of Lords case Lord Cranworth said 'the auditors may be agents of the shareholders as far as relates to the audit of the accounts. For the purposes of the audit, the auditors will bind the shareholders'.

The question of whether the auditor is an *officer* of the company is more problematic. As has already been pointed out, the term 'officer' does not, as defined in the 1948 Act, specifically include the auditor. Yet for the following two reasons it is possible that, for certain purposes anyway, the auditor is to be regarded as an officer:

3

(a) Section 14 (1976) described above speaks of the auditors as holding *'office'*; and

(b) Section 161 (1948) itself states (rather obviously!) that for the purposes of the provision that an officer is disqualified from acting as auditor, the references to 'officer' are *not* to be construed as including the auditor! *This nevertheless suggests that the term officer may include the auditor in some other context.*

As a result of this statutory confusion the courts have from time to time been called upon to decide whether, for a particular purpose, the auditor should be regarded as an officer of the company. This is fully explained in the Appendix to this chapter.

### Rights (or Powers) (Section 14, 1967; Section 18, 1976)

The following constitute the counterpart to the auditor's duties. Duties without the corresponding rights needed to make them effective would clearly be unacceptable:

(a) right to receive notice of all general meetings of the company, *and* to attend such meetings;

(b) right to be heard at all general meetings of the company on any matter which concerns him in his capacity as auditor;

(c) rights associated with a proposal to replace him or remove him from office;

(d) right of access at all times to all books, documents and vouchers of the company;

(e) right to require from the officers of the company such information and explanations as he considers necessary for the purposes of his audit;

(f) right to require subsidiaries and their auditors to provide such information and explanations as may be needed in the course of his duties as parent company auditor.

### Duties (Section 14, 1967)

#### The Report to Members

The most important duty of the statutory auditor is to *report* to the members as required under Section 14 of the 1967 Act. *Every* auditor's report on the accounts of a limited company must state, at the very least, whether in the auditor's opinion:

(a) the balance sheet gives a true and a fair view of the state of the company's affairs at the balance sheet date;

(b) the profit and loss account gives a true and fair view of the profit (or loss) for the period ended on that date; and

(c) the accounts have been properly prepared in accordance with the provisions of the Companies Acts 1948 to 1981. (In the case of group accounts submitted by the holding company, the auditor's opinion must deal with the state of affairs and profit or loss of the company and its subsidiaries dealt with thereby, so far as concerns members of the holding company.)

*But note:* The specific matters which the auditor must consider, and report on *'by exception'* only, are as follows:

(a) Whether, in the auditor's opinion, proper accounting records have been kept by the company, as defined in Section 12 (1976). These records must contain a complete record of:

- purchases and sales of goods, identifying buyers and sellers (except in case of normal retail sales)
- receipts and payments of cash

- assets and liabilities, at all times, which must include a statement of stock held at the end of the year, together with compilations from any detailed stocktakings which have been conducted.

Note also that Section 436 (1948) specifies that where the records are not kept in the form of bound books, adequate precautions shall be taken for guarding against falsification and for facilitating its discovery. The 1976 Act provided that the accounting records of public companies must be preserved for 6 years; for private companies the period is 3 years. There are heavy penalties, including imprisonment, for failure to comply with any of the requirements relating to accounting records.

(b) Whether proper returns, adequate for audit purposes, have been received from branches not visited by him;
(c) Whether the balance sheet and profit and loss account are in agreement with the records;
(d) Whether he has received all information and explanations which he required for the purposes of his audit;
(e) Whether the contents of the directors' report are *consistent* with the financial statements (Sec. 15, 1981).

## Inclusion of Further Information

The following five requirements for *disclosure* of information in published accounts are all supported by a stipulation which requires the information specified to be given in the auditor's report, if not given as required in the accounts themselves, or the notes thereto:

(a) Section 196 (1948) on directors' emoluments;
(b) Sections 54–56 (1980) on loans and quasi-loans to officers;
(c) Section 6 (1967) on emoluments of the chairman, highest paid director, and the number of directors whose total UK emoluments fall within each of the specified bands of £5,000;
(d) Section 7 (1967) on total directors' emoluments waived;
(e) Section 8 (1967) on the number of higher-paid employees whose total UK emoluments fall within each of the bands of £5,000.

## Reports in Prospectuses (4th Schedule, Part II, 1948)

If a company makes an issue of shares or debentures to the public a report must be placed in the prospectus by the company's auditors, giving details of:

(a) profits and losses arising in each of the previous five years;
(b) rates of dividend declared in each of the previous five years in respect of each class of shares for the time being paid up;
(c) assets and liabilities as at the latest balance sheet date.

*Notes:* (i) If the company seeks a Stock Exchange quotation for its shares it will be necessary to comply with the requirements of the Quotations Department of the Council of the Stock Exchange, as set out in the 'yellow book' entitled *The Admission of Securities to Quotation*. These requirements are far more extensive than those of the 4th Schedule (1948).

(ii) The amounts of past profits and losses disclosed should be adjusted by the reporting auditors as they consider necessary, bearing in mind the purpose of the report.

## Resignation (Sections 16 and 17, 1976)

These sections provide for the auditor's resignation during office. A resignation notice will only be effective, however, if it contains either

(a) a statement to the effect that there are no circumstances connected with the resignation which the auditor considers should be brought to the notice of members *or creditors;* or
(b) a statement of such circumstances.

5

Where (b) is appropriate, the auditor may also requisition the directors to *call an extraordinary general meeting* for the purpose of considering the resignation circumstances.

*Note:* It is regrettable that these powers may be exercised by auditors only in the context of their own resignation. It should, incidentally, be noted that this is the *only instance* in UK company law that a responsibility towards creditors is conceded.

### False Statements to Auditors (Section 19, 1976)

Largely as a consequence of the unwholesome disclosures in the 1976 D.o.T. Inspectors' report on *London and County Securities*, it is an offence for any officer of a company to make a materially false statement (either orally or in writing) to the auditor, whether knowingly or recklessly. Penalties of imprisonment and/or fines are specified.

### Accounting Reference Period

This is the technical term for financial year, and it terminates on the *accounting reference date*. Unless companies notify the Registrar otherwise, this date will be deemed to be 31 March in each year, although there are provisions for subsequent change.

### Filing

Audited accounts of public companies must be filed with the Registrar no later than 7 months after the accounting reference date (10 months for private companies). The penalties for late filing are £400 plus £40 per day for *each* director in office on the expiry of the deadline; the company is also liable for heavy default fines, and a notice demanding compliance with filing regulations may be served on directors by the Registrar, a member or a creditor.

### The Companies Act 1980 — Introduction

The subject matter of this Act may be subdivided into sections relating to:

  (a) classification of companies (implementation of the EEC second directive);
  (b) the allotment and maintenance of share capital (also concerned with second directive implementation);
  (c) insider dealings;
  (d) the duties of directors, and provisions relating to loans, quasi-loans and other transactions concerning directors;
  (e) the distribution of dividends (implementation of second directive).

### Loans and Quasi-Loans to Directors

The new provisions on directors' loans are designed to overcome the abuses revealed in successive Department of Trade Reports throughout the seventies, in which major companies adopted 'banking articles', as a result of which loans were made to directors, ostensibly 'within the ordinary course of the company's business'. By this means, the company exploited the exemptions previously included in Section 190 of the Companies Act 1948 (now repealed), a practice to which auditors appeared rarely to take exception. It is worth noting that most auditors will now apply more rigorous criteria to this question, as follows:

6

(a) the amount of the loan should not exceed the amount of a loan typically made to unconnected individuals. Also, if a bank's policy is to lend money only to corporate customers, a loan to a director could hardly be said to be in the ordinary course of its business.

(b) the security required should be equivalent to that required for similar loans made to unconnected individuals.

(c) the interest charged should be at least the lowest rate offered on loans made to unconnected individuals, and should not be 'rolled up' unless it is the company's practice to do so with similar loans.

In practice, clients whose business includes the lending of money may be found making loans to directors which fail to measure up to one or more of the above requirements. Frequently these loans are housing loans which are secured by first or second mortgages, but carry concessionary rates of interest. Where it is known that a client has made loans to directors, the partner responsible for the audit should discuss the situation with the client as a *matter of urgency*.

The partner should advise the client that this does not fall within the firm's interpretation of 'in the ordinary course of business', and remind them of the legal requirement to make disclosure in the accounts of the loans which at the balance sheet date do not fall within the restricted definition (specified in (a), (b), and (c) above). Clients should be strongly urged either to correct the terms of the loans to bring them within this interpretation, or to make the necessary disclosure.

A further abuse commonly found in the past relates to loans made by companies to apparently unconnected outside parties who, in the event, simply recycled the loan to a director otherwise precluded from borrowing in this way. These loans are now included within the definition of 'quasi-loan', as now given in Section 65, and are prohibited in the case of public companies. Further abuses, whereby loans were made to members of directors' families, are also covered by the new provisions.

## Transactions with Directors

Under the 1980 Act (Section 50) a transaction with a director is permitted, provided its value 'is not greater, and the terms on which it is entered into are no more favourable . . . than that or those which it is reasonable to expect the company to have offered to . . . a person of the same financial standing . . . but unconnected with the company.

## Distribution of Dividends

Section 39 provides that a company shall not make a distribution except out of profits available for the purpose, and defines these profits as:

(a) its accumulated, realised profits so far as not previously utilised whether by distribution or capitalisation *less*:

(b) its accumulated, realised losses, so far as not previously written off in a reduction or reorganisation of capital duly made.

Various provisions are made regarding the application of unrealised profits, the measuring of a provision, depreciation of revalued fixed assets, original costs of assets and inability to distinguish whether profits/losses are realised or unrealised. Provisions and capitalised development expenditure are to be treated as realised losses, but additional current cost depreciation may be treated as part of realised profits.

Section 40 permits a public company to make a distribution only when its net assets are not less than the aggregate of its called-up share capital and undistributable reserves, and to the extent that the distribution does not reduce the amount of those assets to less than that aggregate. Undistributable reserves are defined as:

(a) share premium account,
(b) capital redemption reserve,
(c) accumulated unrealised profits, less accumulated unrealised losses (in both cases insofar as not previously used),
(d) any reserve prohibited from distribution by law or the company's memorandum or articles.

Section 43 provides that the right of a company to make a distribution, and the amount of any distribution, is to be determined by reference to accounts complying with specific requirements. The accounts are *the most recent audited accounts*, made up as at the company's accounting reference date, or, if the distribution would not be permitted by reference to these accounts, more recent interim accounts. The accounts must carry an *unqualified audit report* or *a statement in writing*.

This means broadly that either a 'clean' opinion is given for the balance sheet being audited or, in the case of a qualified report, *a written statement* that the qualification is not material in determining the propriety of the company's proposed distribution.


**Effect on Case Law**

It is worth noting that Section 39 effectively repeals the decision in the case of *Ammonia Soda Company v. Chamberlain*, in which it was held that a company may pay a dividend out of profits earned in the current period, despite the fact that past losses have not been made good.

Reporting in 1962, the Jenkins Committee on Company Law Reform observed that a company's life is divided into accounting periods for convenience of reporting, and not for determining whether distributable profits have been earned. It is necessary to consider the availability of distributable reserves over the entire life of a company, from its incorporation to the proposed date of payment of a dividend.

Section 39 also nullifies the effect of the infamous *dicta* in *Dimbula Valley (Ceylon) Tea Company v. Laurie (1962)*, in which Buckley J. permitted the distribution by way of dividend of unrealised revaluation surpluses on the grounds that such sums would be available for distribution to members as bonus shares. The Jenkins Committee recommended that there should be a statutory requirement that capital profits should be realised prior to their distribution, and this has now been implemented under Section 39 of the 1980 Act. Section 39 also contains a convoluted clause which deals with the extra depreciation charge which may arise on the revaluation of a fixed asset, from which it appears that additional CCA depreciation, arising on a revaluation surplus, may paradoxically be treated as part of a company's realised profit for dividend purposes.

Section 40 has the effect of classifying a company's balance sheet so as to distinguish (a) share capital and undistributable reserves; (b) free reserves; and (c) assets less liabilities (net assets). The Section requires that public companies may make a distribution only while there is a positive balance under (b) above, and provided that the effect of the distribution will not create a negative balance under this heading.


**Registration as a Public Company**

If a private company wants to re-register as a public company, then Section 5 will apply. This details the procedures to be followed, which include delivering to the registrar a *written statement by the auditors*, and a copy of the relevant balance sheet with *an unqualified audit report*. The 'written statement' must report on the company's net assets being not less than the aggregate of its called up share capital and undistributable reserves. The term 'unqualified audit report' has a similar meaning to that of Section 43 mentioned above, but in the case of a qualified report a written statement must comment on the net assets rather than the proposed distribution of the company. Similar provisions apply where a joint stock company (i.e. a company formed otherwise than under the Companies Acts) wishes to re-register as a public company.

## Non-cash Consideration for Share Capital

If a public company is involved in a take-over, it will require an independent accountant's report on the value of any non-cash assets which are used as payment for shares. The independent accountant is anyone qualified to be auditor of the company and he must value the non-cash assets himself unless it appears reasonable to accept a valuation made by some other person.

## The Companies Act 1981 and the Auditor

### Auditor's Report

*(a) Small and medium-sized companies*   (Section 7). Small and medium-sized companies (as defined) are allowed to submit modified accounts to the Registrar. In this connection the auditors must:

- (i) provide a report *to the directors* stating whether in their opinion the accounts qualify for the exemptions (Section 7 (6));
- (ii) provide a special report to accompany the accounts lodged with the Registrar stating that in their opinion the exemption requirements are satisfied, and reproducing the full text of the report sent to the members.

*(b) Publication of accounts*   (Section 11). All companies except unlimited companies are required to provide full accounts for their members, and 'small' or 'medium-sized' companies may file modified accounts with the Registrar.

Section 11 is designed to prevent anyone being misled by accounts published in any other way. Its provisions are:

- (i) Any accounts, full or modified, which are published must be accompanied by the 'relevant' auditors' report. This means that published full accounts must be accompanied by the full auditors' report and that published modified accounts must be accompanied by the special auditors' report required by Section 7 of the Companies Act 1981.
- (ii) If a company required to produce group accounts publishes its own accounts it must also publish the group accounts, which may be in modified form if the company is small or medium-sized.
- (iii) Any company publishing an abridged form of its accounts must include a statement that they are not full accounts, indicating also whether full accounts have been delivered to the Registrar and whether the auditors' report on those accounts was qualified. The auditors' report itself must *not* be published with abridged accounts.

Although it is obviously the directors' responsibility to comply with these requirements, auditors should be alert to ensure that their clients do not infringe them.

*(c) Application of auditors' report to directors' report.*   It has always been good auditing practice for the auditor to confirm that the directors' report is consistent with the accounts on which the auditor is reporting. This is now made a statutory requirement by S.15 CA 1981 — the auditors must qualify their report if they are of the opinion that the information given in the auditors' report is not consistent with the company's accounts.

## Dormant Companies (Section 12)

Section 12 of the Companies Act 1981 exempts dormant companies from the obligation to appoint auditors. A company qualifies as dormant for this purpose if it is a 'small' company as defined in Section 8, is not a holding company and has had no 'significant accounting transactions' since the end of the previous financial year.

The procedure is for the company to pass a special resolution that auditors are not to be appointed.

The company is still required to lodge accounts with the Registrar, but instead of an auditors' report a statement from the directors that the company was dormant must be filed.

## Redemption of Redeemable Shares — Private Companies

If a private company redeems shares out of capital, as they are allowed to do by Sections 54 to 58, subject to certain safeguards, the directors must make a statutory declaration of the solvency of the company, accompanied by a report addressed to the directors by the auditors stating that they have inquired into the company's state of affairs, that the amount to be paid out of capital has been properly determined and that the opinion expressed by the directors is reasonable. The statutory declaration and the auditors' report on it must be open for inspection by the members at the meeting to pass the special resolution approving the payment.

## Private Company Purchasing its Own Shares

An auditors' report identical with that described above for redemption of redeemable shares is required to accompany the directors' declaration when a private company purchases its own shares out of capital.

## Private Company Providing Financial Assistance for the Purchase of its Own Shares

Before such assistance can legally be provided the directors must file a statutory declaration of solvency which must again be accompanied by an auditors' report to the directors confirming that they are aware of nothing to indicate that the directors' opinion is unreasonable.

## Treatment of Capitalised Development Costs

Section 84 of the Companies Act 1981 inserts a new Section 42A into the Companies Act 1980. It provides that any capitalised development cost is to be treated as a realised loss for the purpose of determining distributable profit under Section 39 of the 1980 Act, unless the directors are of the opinion that there are special circumstances making it reasonable not to treat that development cost as a realised loss. If the directors are of this opinion they must state so in the note to the accounts required by Para. 20, 8th Schedule.

The provision applies also for the purpose of Section 41 in determining the distributable profit of an investment company.

## Distributions in Kind

Section 85 of the Companies Act 1981 inserts a new Section 43A into the 1980 Act. The new section provides that where a company makes a distribution in kind and the value of the asset distributed includes an unrealised profit, that profit is to be treated as a realised profit for the purpose of determining the legality of the distribution.

## Investigations

(a) Investigation on application of company.   Section 86 extends the provisions of Section 164 of the Companies Act 1948 (investigation of a company's affairs by the Department of Trade on an application by members) to include the ordering of such an investigation at the instance of the company. Formerly, a special resolution was required where the company requested an investigation (Section 165(1)(a)(i) Companies Act 1948) — this subsection no longer has effect (Section 86(3)) so that in future an ordinary resolution of the company or a resolution of the directors will be sufficient.

The security for costs of the investigation which the Department of Trade may require is increased from £100 to £5,000.

*(b) Access to books and documents.* Section 87 adds a new subsection 1A to Section 167 of the 1948 Act, which requires directors and officers to produce books, etc., at an investigation, by enabling inspectors who consider that any other person is or may be in possession of information concerning the company's affairs, to require that person to produce books and documents in his possession relating to the company and to give all reasonable assistance with the investigation.

It also adds a new subsection 1B to the same section enabling the inspector to require a past or present director of a company or its subsidiary or holding company under investigation to produce to him all documents in his possession or under his control relating to his bank account, provided that the inspector thinks on reasonable grounds that payments have been made into or out of the account in respect of:

(a) undisclosed directors' remuneration; or
(b) substantial contracts between companies and their directors or connected persons which by Section 54 of the 1980 Act should have been disclosed in the accounts and were not so disclosed; or
(c) transactions between recognised banks and their directors which do not meet the disclosure requirements of Section 56(4) of the 1980 Act, or particulars of which were not included in the register of transactions provided for by Section 57 of the 1980 Act; or
(d) acts or omissions which constituted misconduct, whether fraudulent or not, towards the company or its subsidiary or holding company or its members under investigation.

This subsection does not extend to investigations under Section 172 of the 1948 Act (see (d) below).

Note that since the decision of the House of Lords in *R. v. IRC, Ex parte Rossminster (1980)* it seems clear beyond doubt that the requirement that the inspector must think 'on reasonable grounds' is to be objectively construed — i.e. there must exist reasonable grounds in fact, and it is not sufficient that the inspector honestly believes in the reasonableness of objectively unreasonable grounds.

*(c) Inspectors' reports.* Section 88(1) substitutes a new Section 168(2) of the 1948 Act to provide that where inspectors were appointed by order of the court under Section 165 of the Companies Act 1948 the Secretary of State is to furnish a copy of the report to the court and may if he thinks fit forward a copy to the company's registered office and provide a copy on request and payment of a fee to (a) any member of the company under investigation, (b) any person whose conduct is referred to in the report, (c) the auditors concerned, (d) the applicants for the investigation and (e) any other person whose financial interest appears to the Secretary of State to be affected by matters dealt with in the report.

Section 88(2) amends Section 171 of the 1948 Act by providing that a copy of the inspectors' report shall be admissible as evidence of the inspectors' opinion provided it is certified by the Secretary of State to be a true copy.

*(d) Department of Trade investigations.* Section 89(b) extends the power of the Department of Trade under Sections 166 to 168 of the 1948 Act, when carrying out an investigation under Section 172 of the 1948 Act of the ownership of a company to any person whom the inspector reasonably believes to possess information relevant to the investigation.

Section 89(c) provides that the Secretary of state may, if he thinks there is good reason for not divulging part of a report, omit that part from disclosure. He may cause the Registrar to keep a copy of the report with that part omitted, or in the case of any other such report, a copy of the whole report.

*(e) Extension of powers to require information.*   Section 90 extends the Department of Trade's powers to require information under Section 173 of the 1948 Act as to persons interested in shares or debentures, to any person having or being able to obtain such information. The section previously applied only to persons interested in shares or debentures or who had acted as solicitor or agent in respect thereof.

*(f) Power to impose restrictions on shares or debentures.*   Section 91 inserts several new sub-sections in Section 174 of the 1948 Act.

The power to impose restrictions is no longer confined to cases where the difficulty in discovering relevant facts is due wholly or mainly to the unwillingness of the persons concerned to assist in the investigation.

Purported agreements to transfer either shares which are subject to a restriction on transfer or rights to be issued with unissued shares which are similarly subject are void.

An aggrieved party may apply to the court for an order that the restrictions be lifted, and such an order may be made if the court is satisfied that the relevant facts have been disclosed to the company and that no unfair advantage accrued to any person as a result of a failure to make disclosure, or the shares are to be sold and the court or the Secretary of State approves the sale (see next paragraph).

The court may direct that any shares which are subject to restrictions under Section 174 of the 1948 Act be sold, subject to the court's approval of the terms of sale, and such restrictions may be lifted in consequence.

*(g) Disclosure of information obtained from certain investigations.*   Section 104 by substituting Section 111(1)(c) to (f), Companies Act 1967, provides that information obtained under Sections 109 or 110 of that Act; or under various other Acts, may be made available to inspectors appointed to conduct formal inspections under Sections 164, 165 or 172, Companies Act 1948, or Section 32, Companies Act 1967, for the purposes of cross-examination of any person in the inspection.

*(h) Professional privilege.*   Section 103 amends various sections of the Companies Acts 1948 and 1967 to extend privilege from the disclosure of information requirements to barristers and advocates as well as to solicitors, save insofar as the name of the lawyer's client is concerned, and to extend the privilege to matters in the hands of the client.

*(i) Investigation by the Department of Trade on a liquidator's report.*   The Department of Trade has power under Section 334(3), Companies Act 1948, to investigate cases where it appears to the liquidator of a company in voluntary winding up that any present or past officer of the company has committed a criminal offence in relation to the company. By Section 92(1) the Department, where a liquidator's report is referred to it by the Director of Public Prosecutions or the Lord Advocate for further inquiry, may exercise all the powers available to inspectors under the general inspection provisions of Section 164 or Section 165, Companies Act, 1948.

### Appendix: The Auditor as an Officer?

This question is of particular concern in connection with the winding-up penalty provisions in Sections 328 to 333 of the Companies Act 1948. The last of these concerns civil offences, but all the others involve criminal offences. All six sections, however, refer to 'any *officer* of a company'.

*Civil Offences: Companies Act 1948, Section 333*

The section is part of the general winding-up provisions under the Companies Act.

Section 333 is concerned with the civil offences entitled *'misfeasance'* and *'breach of trust'*. Broadly speaking, these terms relate to the misuse of a position of authority with the object of personal gain. For example, the directors of a company may bind the company in a contract with an outside party with whom they have an existing financial relationship, i.e. a transaction which is not at arm's length. If a similar contract could have been entered into by the company on more favourable terms, it could be argued that the directors have abused their power and position in order to achieve a personal benefit, at the expense of the company for whom they are acting as stewards. In the event of such an offence being proved, the appropriate remedy would financial damages, making good the loss.

It was decided in the two famous legal cases of *Kingston Cotton Mill* and *London and General Bank* at the end of the last century that for the purposes of the above provisions *the auditor was to be regarded as an officer of the company*.

### Criminal Offences: Companies Act 1948, Sections 328, 329 330 and 332

The other winding-up sections referred to above all involve criminal offences, and in each case reference is made to 'officers' of the company. The question has therefore arisen as to how far, if at all, the auditor may be regarded as being an officer of the company for the purposes of these sections, bearing in mind that the two cases referred to in the previous section related *only* to civil liability.

It was held in the case of *R. v. Shacter (1960)* that the term 'officer' must be taken to include the auditor. In 1953 the appellant was appointed auditor of a company and his appointment was continued from year to year thereafter. He was convicted, as *'an officer'* of the company, of making false entries, fraud and defaults contrary to Sections 328(1)(j), 330 and 331 (now repealed — 1976) of the Companies Act 1948.

# 2 Auditing Standards — 1980

*After a gestation period of two years, the Auditing Practices Committee of the CCAB (Consultative Committee of Accountancy Bodies) produced the first ever set of definitive Auditing Standards. Before considering their content and impact, readers may find a brief historical recapitulation useful in adding perspective to this important development.*

The CCAB, it will be remembered, was the phoenix which rose, somewhat bedraggled, from the ashes of the 1970 integration proposals. It is a loose federation of the six major UK accounting bodies, and its chief activities are channelled through three broadly constituted subcommittees: Parliamentary and Law; Accounting Standards; and Auditing Practices.

The first of these provides a two-way communication link between the profession and the legislature, ensuring (a) that government is familiar with accountants' views on proposed legislation — fiscal and companies in particular, and (b) that the accountants are aware of important developments in parliament and in the law courts. The work of the ASC is familiar to us all, and is amply evidenced by 19 Accounting Standards and 31 exposure drafts — a commendable volume of output in ten years, considering its slender and overworked resources.

The APC, however, has had a somewhat chequered career, spanning the most difficult decade in the profession's 100-year history. These problems have arisen primarily from the country's economic malaise and its inevitable effect on corporate conduct and performance, as manifested in dozens of Department of Trade Inspectors' Reports. Many of these have outlined in graphic terms the difference between the actual contribution made by auditors and public expectation of their rôle. It has thus become abundantly clear that the work of auditors must in future be based on altogether more rigorous standards of objectivity and vigilance, especially when external pressures — arising from fluctuating exchange rates, international competition, runaway inflation and high interest rates — have the combined effect of severely squeezing normal commercial returns.

## From Discussion Drafts to Standards

It was against this background that in May 1978 the first three discussion drafts of Auditing Standards were published, and these dealt respectively with (a) the auditor's 'operational Standard'; (b) the audit report; and (c) qualifications in audit reports. The final versions, now published as official Standards, do not at first glance appear to differ significantly; but such differences as there are should not be underestimated. Indeed, they reflect a good deal of new thinking on the part of their eminent authors, particularly in the formulation of the operational Standard.

In essence, the original discussion draft on this theme was centred on the need for auditors to ascertain and evaluate the reliability of client companies' internal controls as the springboard for all further audit work — i.e. the now familiar 'systems-based' approach, whose origins may be traced to the development in the fifties of the first internal control questionnaires by the major international firms. The logic of this approach rests on the observation that all systems, by definition, incorporate within their scope a measurable degree of 'self-audit', and that it is therefore necessary for external auditors to concentrate their efforts on only those aspects of the system seen to be weak, susceptible to abuse, or otherwise defective in conception/execution. Such efforts would normally take the form of audit tests in volumes sufficient to enable the auditor to form an opinion on the reliability of the records as a basis for the preparation of final accounts.

This familiar method of work is, of course, all very well in cases where the overall level of control is adequate, and encompasses the powers and activities of senior management as well as their subordinates, but this is rarely the case with the vast numbers of smaller private companies, especially those which are proprietorially dominated — directors and shareholders being the same people.

Despite the obvious inapplicability of the 'systems-based' philosophy to such clients, many smaller audit firms have been tempted to 'adapt' standard large firm documentation such as extended working paper indices, voluminous ICQ and ICE forms, and many other audit aids of dubious usefulness in the context of the small company audit. The growth of this tendency, based on a blind 'follow my leader' herd instinct, was attributable to the miguided supposition that impressive audit documentation constitutes some sort of 'insurance policy', and resulted in the creation of so much work on the auditor's own papers that little time was left for any investigation of the client's records! Far from reducing susceptibility to charges of negligence, this practice probably *raised* the level of professional risks.

The draft on the operational Standard therefore performed an invaluable incidental service in forcing auditors serving throughout the professional spectrum to consider carefully whether they genuinely believed that the systems-based approach should become enshrined within the new code of practice — backed up, moreover, by the recently approved and all-pervading disciplinary rules. These threaten those in breach with penalties ranging from public censure (and a fine) to exclusion from membership.

## 'Evidence' Rules — OK?

As a result, the definitive operational Standard completely reverses the emphasis: the search for audit *evidence*, in whatever form may be appropriate, is now of paramount importance; and the presence of effective internal controls represents but one of the many available forms of evidence that the records are reliable, and hence that the accounts show a true and fair view. In its introduction to the Standards, the APC booklet *True and Fair* informs us that the placing of the material on internal control before that on evidence caused 'considerable confusion'. One suspects that the epithet 'revolution' might have been more apt! Nonetheless, all's well that ends well, and the implicit freedom to apply audit skills as the situation demands, which is now effectively built into the Standards, may well represent the beginning of the end of 25 years of rigid adherence to the systems-based approach.

The Standard on the audit report itself incorporates only one major change: departures from accounting Standards with which the auditors concur, as being necessary in order to give a true and fair view, need no longer be specifically referred to in the report. This is a welcome change, since such purely academic references have in the past been misconstrued as qualifications.

## Qualifications in Reports

The Standard on qualified audit reports divides the circumstances of qualification into those involving uncertainty and disagreement respectively, and either situation may be regarded as having an effect on the accounts which is simply 'material' or, more seriously, 'fundamental', in which case the uncertainty or disagreement actually undermines, in the auditors' opinion, the truth and fairness of the view presented, and requires either a disclaimer of an opinion altogether (uncertainty), or an adverse opinion (disagreement). Where, by contrast, the problem is no more than "material" the report may state that the accounts do give a true and fair view "subject to" the specified uncertainty, or "except for" the disagreement in question.

The published Guidelines provide no fewer than 17 specimen reports, covering a wide range of situations, and it is gratifying (but by no means surprising) to find that the infamous Example 7 (in the discussion draft guidelines) has been dropped. This example amply demonstrated what can happen when systems-based audit attitudes are misguidedly applied to the incorporated fish-and-chip shop. It began by complaining of a lack (or inadequacy) of internal control — albeit 'in common with many businesses of similar size and organization' — and pointed out that such a lack 'prevented us from carrying out the audit procedures which we considered necessary'.

This formulation clearly conjures up an image of auditors marching in, forearmed with an array of potential audit procedures, only to be bitterly frustrated by finding nothing on which to lavish their preconceived notions. This ingenious specimen, which would probably have had to be appended to the accounts of some 200,000 companies, concluded with a disclaimer of any opinion at all.

The new guidelines now incorporate a far more intelligent example which simply observes that (a) the controls are dependent upon the close involvement of the director(s), and (b) where no independent evidence was available to support recorded transactions, the auditors relied to a large degree upon management assurances. The report sensibly concludes that 'subject to' these circumstances the accounts, in the auditors' opinion, give a true and fair view.

Although clearly preferable to the travesty of the reporting art which it replaces, even this version has its dangers. The circumstances to which it refers could, for example, be construed as giving the auditors an excuse for simply accepting management assurances as a substitute for deeper investigation. Important though such assurances are, it is dangerous in the extreme to accept them without also seeking the corroborative evidence of ratios, trends, and comparisons with earlier periods and other similar businesses; procedures to which the report makes no reference. It may indeed be thought unwise to fill the report with detailed matter relating to audit procedures — but not, in the view of some, nearly so unwise as telling only part of the story, and possibly creating a false impression in the process.

Readers should note that the mandatory application of auditing Standards to professional work applies to the concise subject matter of the Standards alone — not the Guidelines. For example, the second paragraph of the operational Standard requires auditors to 'plan, control and record' their work. The Guideline to this outlines several of the methods which auditors may use in practice with a view to ensuring that audit assignments are adequately planned, controlled, etc. There is no intention that the subject matter of the Guidelines should occupy any greater status than their counterpart appendices to Accounting Standards, which are included purely as illustrative material and do not form part of the Standards themselves.

The full text of the Standards is as follows.


**The Auditor's Operational Standard**

1. This auditing standard applies whenever an audit is carried out.

*Planning, Controlling and Recording*

2. The auditor should adequately plan, control and record his work.

*Accounting Systems*

3. The auditor should ascertain the enterprise's system of recording and processing transactions and assess its adequacy as a basis for the preparation of financial statements.

*Audit Evidence*

4. The auditor should obtain relevant and reliable audit evidence sufficient to enable him to draw reasonable conclusions therefrom.

16

*Internal Control*

5. If the auditor wishes to place reliance on any internal controls he should ascertain and evaluate those controls and perform compliance tests on their operation.

*Review of Financial Statements*

6. The auditor should carry out such a review of the financial statements as is sufficient, in conjunction with the conclusions drawn from the other audit evidence obtained, to give him a reasonable basis for his opinion on the financial statements.

*Effective Date*

7. This Auditing Standard is effective for the audit of financial statements relating to accounting periods starting on or after 1 April 1980.

## The Audit Report

1. This Auditing Standard applies to all reports in which the auditor expresses an opinion on financial statements intended to give a true and fair view of the state of affairs, profit or loss and, where applicable, source and application of funds. The Standard is not intended to override the statutory exemptions granted in respect of certain types of enterprise but is intended to apply to the audit reports relating to such enterprises in other respects.
2. The audit report should identify those to whom it is addressed and the financial statements to which it relates.
3. The auditor should refer expressly in his report to the following:

    (a) whether the financial statements have been audited in accordance with approved Auditing Standards;
    (b) whether in the auditor's opinion the financial statements give a true and fair view of the state of affairs, profit or loss and, where applicable, source and application of funds; and
    (c) any matters prescribed by relevant legislation or other requirements.

*Effective Date*

4. This Auditing Standard is effective for the audit of financial statements relating to accounting periods starting on or after 1 April 1980.

## Qualifications in Audit Reports

1. When the auditor is unable to report affirmatively on the matters contained in paragraph 3 of the Auditing Standard 'The Audit Report', he should qualify his report by referring to all material matters about which he has reservations. All reasons for the qualification should be given, together with a quantification of its effect on the financial statements if this is both relevant and practicable. Additionally, reference may need to be made to non-compliance with relevant legislation and other requirements.
2. A qualified audit report should leave the reader in no doubt as to its meaning and its implications for an understanding of the financial statements. To promote a more consistent understanding of qualified reports the forms of qualification described in this standard should be used unless, in the auditor's opinion, to do so would fail to convey clearly the intended meaning.
3. The nature of the circumstances giving rise to the qualification of opinion will generally fall into one of two categories:

**Table 1**

| Nature of circumstances | Material but not fundamental | Fundamental |
|---|---|---|
| Uncertainty | 'SUBJECT TO' OPINION | DISCLAIMER OF OPINION |
| Disagreement | 'EXCEPT' OPINION | ADVERSE OPINION |

    (a) where there is an uncertainty which prevents the auditor from forming an opinion on a matter (uncertainty); or

    (b) where the auditor is able to form an opinion on a matter but this conflicts with the view given by the financial statements (disagreement).

Each of these categories gives rise to alternative forms of qualification depending upon whether the subject matter of the uncertainty or disagreement is considered to be fundamental so as to undermine the view given by the financial statements taken as a whole.

4. The forms of qualification which should be used in different circumstances (Table 1) are:

    (a) In a disclaimer of opinion the auditor states that he is unable to form an opinion as to whether the financial statements give a true and fair view.

    (b) In an adverse opinion the auditor states that in his opinion the financial statements do not give a true and fair view.

    (c) In a 'subject to' opinion the auditor effectively disclaims an opinion on a particular matter which is not considered fundamental.

    (d) In an 'except' opinion the auditor expresses an adverse opinion on a particular matter which is not considered fundamental.

*Effective Date*

5. This Auditing Standard is effective for the audit of financial statements relating to accounting periods starting on or after 1 April 1980.

**Examples of Audit Reports**

Although the scope of this book does not allow for the reproduction of all the Guidelines in full, certain of the examples of audit reports are included so that students may gain a sense of the type of formulation which in future will satisfy the requirements laid down by the second and third Standards.

*Example 1    Unqualified Audit Report: Companies without Subsidiaries — Great Britain*

AUDITORS' REPORT TO THE MEMBERS OF

We have audited the financial statements on pages . . . to . . . in accordance with approved Auditing Standards.

    In our opinion the financial statements, which have been prepared under the historical cost convention as modified by the revaluation of land and buildings, give a true and fair view of the state of the company's affairs at 31 December 19.. and of its profit and source and application of funds for the year then ended and comply with the Companies Acts 1948 to 1981.

*Example 2    Unqualified Audit Report: Companies Submitting Group Accounts — Great Britain*

AUDITORS' REPORT TO THE MEMBERS OF

We have audited the financial statements on pages . . . to . . . in accordance with approved Auditing Standards.

In our opinion the financial statements, which have been prepared under the historical cost convention as modified by the revaluation of land and buildings, give a true and fair view of the state of affairs of the company and the group at 31 December 19.. and of the profit and source and application of funds of the group for the year then ended and comply with the Companies Acts 1948 to 1981.

*Example 5    Qualified Audit Report: Uncertainty — Subject to: No Stock Count at a Branch*

AUDITORS' REPORT TO THE MEMBERS OF

We have audited the financial statements on pages . . . to . . . Our audit was conducted in accordance with approved Auditing Standards except that the scope of our work was limited by the matter referred to below.

One branch of the company did not carry out a physical count of stock at 31 December 19.. and there were no practicable alternative auditing procedures that we could apply to confirm quantities. Accordingly, we have been unable to obtain all the information and explanations considered necessary to ourselves as to the existence of stock valued at £ . . . at 31 December 19.. which is included as part of the total stock of £ . . . in the balance sheet. In our opinion, in the case of the stocks referred to above, proper accounting records have not been kept as required by Section 12, Companies Act 1976.

Subject to the effects of any adjustments which might have been shown to be necessary had a physical count of branch stock been carried out, in our opinion the financial statements, which have been prepared under the historical cost convention, give a true and fair view of the state of the company's affairs at 31 December 19.. and of its profit and source and application of funds for the year then ended and comply with the Companies Acts 1948 to 1981.

*Example 6    Qualified Audit Report: Uncertainty — Subject to: Acceptance of Management Assurances (Small Business)*

AUDITORS' REPORT TO THE MEMBERS OF

We have audited the financial statements on pages . . . to . . . Our audit was conducted in accordance with approved Auditing Standards having regard to the matters referred to in the following paragraph.

In common with many businesses of similar size and organisation the company's system of control is dependent upon the close involvement of the directors/managing director, [who are major shareholders]. Where independent confirmation of the completeness of the accounting records was therefore not available we have accepted assurances from the directors/managing director that all the company's transactions have been reflected in the records.

Subject to the foregoing, in our opinion the financial statements, which have been prepared under the historical cost convention, give a true and fair view of the state of the company's affairs at 31 December 19.. and of its profit and source and application of funds for the year then ended and comply with the Companies Acts 1948 to 1981.

*Example 7    Qualified Audit Report: Uncertainty — Subject to: Going Concern*

AUDITORS' REPORT TO THE MEMBERS OF

We have audited the financial statements on pages . . . to . . . in accordance with approved Auditing Standards.

As stated in note . . . the company is currently negotiating for long-term facilities to replace the loan of £. . . which becomes repayable on (a date early in the next financial year); continuation of the company's activities is dependent upon a successful outcome to these negotiations. The financial statements have been drawn up on a going concern basis which assumes that adequate facilities will be obtained.

Subject to a satisfactory outcome of the negotiations referred to above, in our opinion the financial statements, which have been prepared under the historical cost convention, give a true and fair view of the state of affairs of the company and the group at 31 December 19.. and of the profit and source and application of funds of the group for the year then ended and comply with the Companies Acts 1948 to 1981.

*Example 9   Qualified Audit Report: Uncertainty — Disclaimer: Accounting Breakdown*

AUDITORS' REPORT TO THE MEMBERS OF

We have audited the financial statements on pages . . . to  . . . Our audit was conducted in accordance with approved Auditing Standards except that the scope of our work was limited by the matter referred to below.

As stated in note . . ., a fire at the company's computer centre destroyed many of accounting records. The financial statements consequently include significant amounts based on estimates. In these circumstances we were unable to carry out all the auditing procedures, or to obtain all the information and explanations we considered necessary.

Because of the significance of the matter referred to in the preceding paragraph, we are unable to form an opinion as to (i) whether the financial statements give a true and fair view of the state of the company's affairs as at 31 December 19.. and of its profit and source and application of funds for the year then ended, (ii) whether proper accounting records have been kept, or (iii) whether the financial statements comply in all respects with the Companies Acts 1948 to 1981.

*Example 12   Qualified Audit Report: Disagreement — Except: Failure to Apply SSAP 4*

AUDITORS' REPORT TO THE MEMBERS OF

We have audited the financial statements on pages . . . to . . . in accordance with approved Auditing Standards.

As explained in note . . . Regional Development Grants have been credited in full to profits instead of being spread over the lives of the relevant assets as required by Statement of Standard Accounting Practice No. 4; the effect of so doing has been to increase group profits before and after taxation for the year by £. . . (19.. £. . .).

Except for the effects of accounting for Regional Development Grants in the manner described in the preceding paragraph, in our opinion the financial statements, which have been prepared under the historical cost convention, give a true and fair view of the state of affairs of the company and the group at 31 December 19.. and of the profit and source and application of funds of the group for the year then ended and comply with the Companies Acts 1948 to 1981.

*Example 15   Qualified Audit Report: Disagreement — Adverse Opinion: Contract Losses Not Provided For in Accordance with SSAP 9*

AUDITORS' REPORT TO THE MEMBERS OF

We have audited the financial statements on pages . . . to . . . in accordance with approved Auditing Standards.

As more fully explained in note . . . no provision has been made for losses expected to arise on certain long-term contracts currently in progress because the directors consider that such losses should be offset against expected but unearned future profits on other long-term contracts. In our opinion provision should be made for foreseeable losses on individual contracts as required by Statement of Standard Accounting Practice No. 9. If losses had been so recognised the effect would have been to reduce the profit before and after tax for the year and the contract work in progress at 31 December 19.. by £. . . .

In view of the significant effect of the failure to provide for the losses referred to above, in our opinion the financial statements do not give a true and fair view of the state of the company's affairs at 31 December 19.. and of its profit and source and application of funds for the year then ended.

In other respects the financial statements in our opinion comply with the Companies Acts 1948 to 1981.

**Audit Evidence**

The Guidelines to the operational Standard are extremely forthcoming and to some extent duplicate the subject matter included in most modern Auditing texts, so far as procedural matters are concerned. In view of the emphasis placed in this Standard upon audit evidence, the Guideline on this subject is reproduced below. It is emphasised that this chapter is designed to acquaint students as much with the philosophy underlying the new Standards as with the most important aspects of their content. There is, however, no substitute for a thorough study being made of the full text of the Standards and Guidelines themselves.

*Introduction*

1. Paragraph 4 of the Auditing Standard, *The Auditor's Operational Standard*, states that: 'The auditor should obtain relevant and reliable audit evidence sufficient to enable him to draw reasonable conclusions therefrom'.

This Auditing Guideline, which gives guidance on how that paragraph may be applied, should be read in conjunction with the Explanatory Foreword to Auditing Standards and Guidelines including the Glossary of Terms.

*Background*

2. *The nature of audit evidence.* Audit evidence is information obtained by the auditor in arriving at the conclusions on which he bases his opinion on the financial statements. Sources of audit evidence include the accounting and underlying documentation of the enterprise, its tangible assets, management and employees, its customers, suppliers and other third parties who have dealings with, or knowledge of, the enterprise or its business.
3. The sources and amount of evidence needed to achieve the required level of assurances are questions for the auditor to determine by exercising his judgement in the light of the opinion called for under the terms of his engagement. He will be influenced by the materiality of the matter being examined, the relevance and reliability of evidence available from each source and the cost and time involved in obtaining it. Often the auditor will obtain evidence from several sources which, together, will provide him with the necessary assurance.
4. *Sufficiency.* The auditor can rarely be certain of the validity of the financial statements. However, he needs to obtain sufficient relevant and reliable evidence to form a reasonable basis for his opinion thereon. The auditor's judgement as to what constitutes sufficient, relevant and reliable audit evidence is influenced by such factors as:
   (a) his knowledge of the business of the enterprise and the industry in which it operates;
   (b) the degree of risk of misstatement through errors or irregularities; this risk may be affected by such factors as:
      (i) the nature and materiality of the items in the financial statements;
      (ii) the auditor's experience as to the reliability of the management and staff of the enterprise and of its records;
      (iii) the financial position of the enterprise;
      (iv) possible management bias.

5. *Relevance.* The relevance of the audit evidence should be considered in relation to the overall audit objective of forming an opinion and reporting on the financial statements. To achieve this objective the auditor needs to obtain evidence to enable him to draw reasonable conclusions in answer to the following questions.

*Balance Sheet Items*

(a) Have all of the assets and liabilities been recorded?

(b) Do the recorded assets and liabilities exist?

(c) Are the assets owned by the enterprise and are the liabilities properly those of the enterprise?

(d) Have the amounts attributed to the assets and liabilities been arrived at in accordance with the stated accounting policies, on an acceptable and consistent basis?

(e) Have the assets, liabilities and capital and reserves been properly disclosed?

*Profit and Loss Account Items*

(f) Have all income and expenses been recorded?

(g) Did the recorded income and expense transactions in fact occur?

(h) Have the income and expenses been measured in accordance with the stated accounting policies, on an acceptable and consistent basis?

(i) have income and expenses been properly disclosed where appropriate?

6. *Reliability*. Although the reliability of audit evidence is dependent upon the particular circumstances, the following general presumptions may be found helpful:

(a) documentary evidence is more reliable than oral evidence;

(b) evidence obtained from independent sources outside the enterprise is more reliable than that secured solely from within the enterprise;

(c) evidence originated by the auditor by such means as analysis and physical inspection is more reliable than evidence obtained from others.

7. The auditor should consider whether the conclusions drawn from different types of evidence are consistent with one another. When audit evidence obtained from one source appears inconsistent with that obtained from another, the reliability of each remains in doubt until further work has been done to resolve the inconsistency. However, when the individual items of evidence relating to particular matter are all consistent, then the auditor may obtain a cumulative degree of assurance higher than that which he obtains from the individual items.

## Procedures

8. *Obtaining audit evidence*. Audit evidence is obtained by carrying out audit tests which may be classified as 'substantive' or 'compliance' according to their primary purpose. Both such purposes are sometimes achieved concurrently. Substantive tests are defined as those tests of transactions and balances, and other procedures such as analytical review, which seek to provide audit evidence as to the completeness, accuracy and validity of the information contained in the accounting records or in the financial statements. Compliance tests are defined as those tests which seek to provide audit evidence that internal control procedures are being applied as prescribed.

9. The auditor may rely on appropriate evidence obtained by substantive testing to form his opinion, provided that sufficient of such evidence is obtained. Alternatively, he may be able to obtain assurance from the presence of reliable system of internal control, and thereby reduce the extent of substantive testing. The audit procedures which are appropriate when the auditor wishes to place reliance on the enterprise's internal controls are set out in the Auditing Guideline *Internal Controls*.

## Techniques of Audit Testing

10. Techniques of audit testing fall into the following broad categories:

(a) *Inspection* — reviewing or examining records, documents or tangible assets. Inspection of records and documents provides evidence of varying degrees of reliability depending upon their nature and source (see paragraph 6b above). Inspection of tangible assets provides the auditor with reliable evidence as to their existence, but not necessarily as to their ownership, cost or value.

(b) *Observation* — looking at an operation or procedure being performed by others with a view to determining the manner of its performance. Observation provides reliable evidence as to the manner of the performance at the time of observation, but not at any other time.

(c) *Enquiry* — seeking relevant information from knowledgeable persons inside or outside the enterprise, whether formally or informally, orally or in writing. The degree of reliability that the auditor attaches to evidence obtained in this manner is dependent on his opinion of the competence, experience, independence and integrity of the respondent.

(d) *Computation* — checking the arithmetical accuracy of accounting records or performing independent calculations.

11. *Analytical review procedures.* In addition to the above techniques, there are analytical review procedures, referred to in paragraph 8 above. These procedures include significant ratios, trends and other statistics and investigating any unusual or unexpected variations. The precise nature of these procedures and the manner in which they are documented will depend on the circumstances of each audit.

12. The comparisons which can be made will depend on the nature, accessibility and relevance of the data available. Once the auditor has decided on the comparisons which he intends to make in performing his analytical review, he should determine what variations he expects to be disclosed by them.

13. Unusual or unexpected variations, and expected variations which fail to occur, should be investigated. Explanations obtained should be verified and evaluated by the auditor to determine whether they are consistent with his understanding of the business and his general knowledge. Explanations may indicate a change in the business of which the auditor was previously unaware in which case he should reconsider the adequacy of his audit approach. Alternatively they may indicate the possibility of misstatements in the financial statements; in these circumstances the auditor will need to extend his testing to determine whether the financial statements do include material misstatements.

**Withdrawn Material**

Partly as a result of the advent of the new Standards certain statements in the Institute's Members' Handbook, previously issued for the guidance of members, have now been withdrawn. New Accounting Standards and recent external developments have also taken their toll on subject matter previously included within the Member's Handbook. A full list of material now withdrawn is given in Table 2.

**Table 2**

| Section reference | Statements | Section reference | Statements |
|---|---|---|---|
| *N 9* | Depreciation of fixed assets | *U 4* | Internal control |
| *N 17* | Events occurring after the balance sheet date | *U 10* | Auditors' reports: forms and qualifications |
| *N 18* | Presentation of balance sheet and profit and loss account | *U 12* | Auditors' working papers |
| *N 20* | Treatment of investments in the balance sheets of trading companies | *U 17* | The effect of Statements of Standard Accounting Practice on auditors' reports |
| *N 23* | Hire purchase, credit sale and rental transactions | *U 18* | Audit problems of the smaller company |
| *N 25* | The accounting treatment of major changes in the sterling parity of overseas currencies | *U 19* | The audit of current purchasing power statements |
| *N 26* | Land Commission Act 1967: accounting implications | *U 20* | Inflation accounting—auditors' reports during the interim period |
| *N 27* | Treatment of taxation in accounts of companies | *U 23* | Auditors' reports on statements of source and application of funds |
| | | *U 25* | Inflation accounting—audit implications of the interim recommendation by the Accounting Standards Committee |
| *S 2* | Notes on statistics relating to income of and capital employed by companies | | |
| *S 6* | Terms used in published accounts of limited companies | *V 1* | Accounting implications of the Redundancy Payments Act 1965 |
| *S 7* | Notes on the preparation and presentation of accounts from incomplete records | *V 11* | Cheques |
| | | *V 13* | Local Government Acts |
| *S 17* | Stock Exchange | *V 15* | Solicitors' accounts |
| *S 22* | Inflation accounting—an interim recommendation by the Accounting Standards Committee | *V 20* | The Counter-Inflation Act 1973: accounting and auditing implications |
| | | *V 21* | Accounting for tax relief on increase in stock values |
| *U 1* | General principles of auditing | *V 23* | Accounting for tax relief on increases in stock values |

# 3 Independence and Professional Ethics

*Although the topics selected for the first published Auditing Standards (see Chapter 2) required definitive treatment in the manner chosen, many commentators would argue that more appropriate themes on which to launch new Standards would have related to standards of training and competence; and standards of independence. Although it is expected that these matters will be covered in due course, the question of independence represents a recurring problem.*

### Independence Rules

The most recent CCAB guidance statement on professional ethics lists the ways in which independence may be lost, and provides guidelines on compromising situations which should be avoided. The following are listed:

(a) Recurring fees receivable from any one source make up an unduly heavy proportion of the auditor's total fee income. The ethics document suggests a limit of 15%.

(b) The auditor is a shareholder or debenture holder of the company whose accounts he is auditing. This and situations (c) and (d) below should be avoided;

(c) The auditor is a blood relation of one or more of the client company's officers;

(d) The auditor is financially involved, personally, with one or more of the client company's officers;

(e) The auditor, in his capacity as financial adviser of a company in severe financial difficulties, is searching for ways of keeping the company 'afloat', yet knows the heavily qualified audit report which is appropriate in the circumstances will render all attempts to salvage the company useless.

*Note 1:*  Auditors are permitted to hold shares in a non-beneficial capacity (e.g. as trustee) provided the holding does not exceed 10% of the trust itself, nor 10% of the class of shares held.

*Note 2:*  Many firms of accountants operate 'independence' rules internally, e.g. forbidding audit staff to deal in the shares of client companies, whether or not they are personally engaged on the audit work. The Companies Act 1980 now forbids this under 'Insider' legislation.

*Note 3:*  It is most important to appreciate that the question of independence is also affected by factors quite outside of the auditor's control. For example, as will be seen when the rights, powers and duties of the statutory auditor are considered it is permissible for directors with a controlling influence to remove the auditor without good cause (possibly with bad cause), and against which act the auditor possesses little effective recourse. Until the auditor is adequately protected against unwarranted dismissal it is difficult to envisage complete independence.

*Note 4:*  So far as small companies are concerned, it is often argued that the independence of auditors is both impossible and unnecessary in view of the fact that shareholders and directors are often the same people. For a fuller discussion of this view, reference should be made to chapter 11.

### Professional Discipline

In recent years, the professional accounting bodies have revised their ethical guidelines with a view to enhancing audit independence — at least so far as the public image is concerned — as an important aspect of the self-regulatory process. 84% of members voting at the Institute's Annual General Meeting in July 1979 (albeit a very small percentage of the total membership) approved the latest revision of the rules of professional conduct. In essence, disciplinary supervision now extends to instances of substandard work, as well as to the more usual areas of misconduct (e.g. failure to attend promptly to correspondence, etc.), and a number of instances have been publicised in the professional press concerning, for example, the issue by auditors of clean reports in circumstances where qualification (on doubts concerning stock valuation, non-compliance with SSAPs, failure to provide a funds statement, to name a few issues) was thought to be more appropriate.

Apart from publication of names of those censured, which may include the firm as well as the individual concerned, fines of up to £1,000 may be levied; practising certificates may be withdrawn for a specified period; and exclusion of membership always exists as an ultimate possibility in severe cases.

Also within the broad context of self-regulation may be seen the specific rules on independence of auditors. Those now preclude all forms of financial and personal entanglement arising from share holdings, loans, relationships in a personal or advisory capacity with company officers, and a situation in which more than 15% of a firm's gross recurring fees are derived from one client source, groups of companies being treated as one for this purpose. Although the initial draft of this guide forbade all shareholdings, the version finally approved permits auditors to act in a non-beneficial trustee capacity as shareholders, provided the shares held do not exceed 10% of the class of shares issued, and do not exceed more than 10% in value of the total trust fund.

While the establishment of these rules is both timely and necessary, it is most important that students of the subject should not overlook the greatest of all impediments to audit independence — the audit fee itself. This remains true irrespective of whether that fee is more or less than 15% of the total. This is not to suggest, however, as some commentators believe, that self-regulation is ultimately impossible and that all audits should be a function of the State, exercised through the offices of the Department of Trade; such a change would involve no improvement in the quality of audits, which would additionally be hamstrung by the usual impost of bureaucratic processes to which all state-sector activities are subject.

There can be no objection to auditors' working for a fee, and there is no need for this fee in any way to compromise the auditors' independence; but under the present arrangements it is the power of the directors to threaten the auditors with removal (in circumstances where, perhaps, they are doing too good a job) that creates the independence problem. There have been far too many cases arising over the past ten years in which it was obvious that, as a result of such threats, spoken or unspoken, auditors have allowed accounts to be published in which there is less than adequate disclosure of all the reservations in the auditors' minds. It is therefore clear that the next step in the enhancement of audit independence must be on the statutory level, in such manner as will allow auditors a right of appeal to an independent body, i.e. incorporating Department of Trade officials as well as members of the professional Institutes, in any circumstances where their proposed removal can be attributed to unworthy motives of the kind alluded to above.

# 4 Auditors' Liability

*In view of the uncertainty which prevails in relation to auditors' liability arising outside of contract (i.e. to third parties), developments in this area of the law should be closely watched. The notes which follow summarise the background of case law leading to the important House of Lords case of* Arenson v. Casson Beckman Rutley & Co, *the outcome of which has important implications for auditors acting as share valuation experts. The auditors claimed that, as arbitrators, they were acting in a 'quasi-judicial' capacity and, provided there was no dishonesty, they therefore had no case to answer. This view was rejected by the House of Lords on appeal and it therefore became necessary for the auditors to make a defence against the allegations of the plaintiff. This third party case history extends to two major decisions in 1981 and 1982, and is followed by a section on responsibility for discovery of fraud.*

## Background

Liability to third parties in respect of physical injury has a long and well established legal history. Most students will be aware of the case of *Donoghue v. Stevenson (1932)* in which damages were awarded in favour of the young lady who consumed the contents of a gingerbeer bottle in a seaside cafe only to be made aware, too late, that such contents included the decomposed remains of a snail! Although the contractual relationship was between her and the vendor of the bottle, damages were awarded against the manufacturers, with whom there was no privity of contract.

Similarly, in *Grant v. Australian Knitting Mills*, the plaintiff was awarded damages in respect of a skin irritation suffered due to a defect in the underwear which he had acquired from a retailer; the damages were awarded against the manufacturer and not the retailer.

Legal cases relating to third party liability for *financial* (as opposed to physical) injury is by no means as consistent.

In the House of Lords case in 1951 of *Candler v. Crane Christmas & Co.*, the majority verdict of their lordships (Lord Denning dissenting) decided that there could be no liability in the absence of a contractual relationship. This decision was reached despite the fact that Mr. Candler had been induced to invest sums in a company on the strength of a set of draft accounts negligently prepared by the company's auditors, acting in their capacity as accountants. The auditors knew that this was the purpose of the accounts which they had been asked to prepare, and did not deny that they had been negligent in executing this assignment.

## The Hedley Byrne Case

The Lords took a totally different view in the 1963 case of *Hedley Byrne & Co. Ltd. v. Heller & Partners Ltd.*, in which they held that the *Candler* case had been wrongly decided. In the 1963 case, a certificate of creditworthiness had been negligently issued by a firm of merchant bankers in response to a request from an outside company; the certificate related to the financial standing of one of the bank's customers.

The Lords decided that since it was quite clear that such a certificate issued in a professional capacity would be relied upon by the party to whom it was issued, the absence of privity did not constitute a valid defence in a negligence claim. Heller & Partners Ltd. nevertheless escaped without having to pay any damages, but purely on the grounds that they had included a clause with the certificate specifically disclaiming responsibility for the consequences of reliance upon such statement. It is therefore clear that they escaped liability by virtue of this disclaimer, rather than the absence of contractual relationship.

The Institute of Chartered Accountants in England and Wales in 1966, following the *Hedley Byrne* decision, sought Counsel's opinion as to how far such liability might extend, and in reaching an opinion Counsel paid particular attention to other cases decided abroad, notably *Ultramares Corporation v. Touche & Co. (New York, 1932)*. In this case, the judge decreed that it would be quite wrong for the auditor to be liable for an indeterminate amount, to an indeterminate class of people, for an indeterminate period of time, and that it was therefore essential that some limitation be placed upon potential liability in the absence of contract.

Counsel's opinion may be summarised in the following way. Liability to a third party in respect of a document or statement would arise only if the following criteria are fulfilled:

(a) there is a clear case of negligence;
(b) financial loss has resulted;
(c) it is clear that the financial loss is attributable to reliance upon the negligently prepared document, etc., and to no other cause;
(d) the party issuing the document, etc., knew the purpose for which it was being prepared, and knew that it was to be relied upon in that particular context.

As a consequence, Counsel put forward the view that liability to shareholders would *not extend to the consequences of their reliance upon the audit report, etc., in the context of an investment decision*, since it is not the purpose of accounts prepared under statute (or of the auditor's report attached thereto) to assist existing or potential shareholders in exercising an investment decision. Such accounts are prepared for *stewardship* purposes only, within the confines of companies legislation, and these accounts, together with the auditor's report, are therefore addressed to existing shareholders only.

It is extremely dubious as to whether this view expressed by Counsel is of any validity today since it is difficult to see what a potential investor (or an existing shareholder contemplating further investment or disinvestment) would rely upon to assist such a decision, if not the published accounts and auditor's report. Until 'The Corporate Report' becomes a reality and separate accounts are prepared specifically for investment purposes in the ordinary course of events, the statutory published accounts have to fulfil a wide variety of functions, to many of which they are ill-suited.

Counsel stated, perhaps equally questionably, that liability to the Inland Revenue could be difficult to prove in a third party context since any tax loss is always recoverable, and any permanent loss would therefore be attributable to the death or decamping of the taxpayer.

The *Hedley Byrne* decision has been followed in a number of cases in recent years. In the Canadian case of *Myers v. Thompson & London Life Insurance Co. (1967)*, an insurance agent failed to see that his insurance company carried out the instructions of the plaintiff's solicitor for surrender of the plaintiff's term policy and issue of a new one to his wife. Thus, when the plaintiff died shortly after, a part of the insurance proceeds was taxed in his estate. Following *Hedley Byrne*, the agent was held personally responsible, for he knew that reliance was being placed on him and his negligence caused the loss to the estate through his failure to exercise the implied duty of care.

More recently, in Australia, in *Evatt v. Citizens and Mutual Life Assurance Co. Ltd.*, the *Hedley Byrne* decision was further restricted to situations in which the issue of the negligent opinion, etc., arises *in the ordinary course of the issuing party's business*. In the *Evatt* case, the parent company of an insurance group negligently gave Mr. Evatt an opinion on the financial standing of one of its subsidiaries, and Mr. Evatt lost heavily as a result of such reliance. The Privy Counsel of the House of Lords held, on appeal, that the opinion had been issued honestly, the company believing it to be true, and, since there was no contractual relationship between the litigating parties, there was no cause for action as the statement was made outside of the ordinary course of the parent company's business.

28

## Auditor as Arbitrator

Late in 1975, the House of Lords held, in *Arenson v. Casson Beckman, Rutley & Co.*, that an accountant or auditor of a private company who, on request, values shares in the company in the knowledge that his valuation is to determine the price to be paid for them under a contract for their sale, may be liable to be sued if he makes his valuation negligently.

In April 1970, Mr. Arenson's employment in his uncle's company was terminated. He and his uncle asked the company's auditors, Cassons, to determine the 'fair value' of his shares in the company as at 4 April. The value given was £4,916. On 11 June, Mr. Arenson, relying on that valuation, transferred his shares to his uncle at £4,916.

In September 1970, a holding company, A. Arenson (Holdings) Ltd., was incorporated to acquire the company's issued share capital; and in 1971 the shares of the holding company were offered to the public on the basis of a valuation jointly prepared by Cassons and another firm of accountants which, if applied pro rata, would allegedly have given Mr. Arenson's shares a value *six* times what he had received for them.

He issued a writ claiming, among other things, that Cassons' valuation was not binding on him; that a fresh valuation should be made; and that his uncle should pay him the true worth of the shares; and alternatively that Cassons were 'negligent in making the valuation'.

This case was of particular importance since it dealt with an unusual aspect of third party liability, i.e. where the defendant has acted in the capacity of an *arbitrator*, holding the scales of equity between disputing parties (who had failed to agree on a valuation on their own). The House of Lords decided that, despite appearances that Cassons had acted in a quasi-judicial capacity, and might thus expect to be entitled to a qualified privilege or immunity from action, they were fully answerable to the plaintiff for the valuation originally determined by them. As a consequence, the case was returned to the lower court for the purpose of determining whether or not negligence had taken place, and if so the extent of the appropriate damages.

An important side-effect of this decision for auditors is the need for them to maintain total secrecy as to their method of arriving at share valuations, and of the computations supporting the valuation; only the final figure should actually be supplied. In this way it would be virtually impossible for any party validly to contest a valuation of shares which, in any event, are notoriously difficult to value — even within a range of amounts. Once a valuation basis and supporting computation is supplied, however, it is always possible for another 'expert' to provide evidence as to why such value is 'defective'.

While on the question of auditors' liability, it should be noted that the majority of such instances are now settled out of court, leaving the amounts involved to the insurance companies to provide, under increasingly expensive professional indemnity policies. The unfortunate effect of this situation is that there is now very little developing case law on this subject, and it is highly probable that in thus seeking blanket cover against all professional risks, firms are insuring to an unreasonable degree — i.e. against a level of liability which, in all likelihood, the English courts would regard as unwarranted.


## The Risk of 'Class Actions'

Writing in the May 1980 issue of *Accountancy*, the author dealt with a new development in potential liability of auditors to third parties, of which the following is an appropriate extract. Although neither the case of *Wallersteiner v. Moir* nor that of *The Prudential Assurance Company v. Newman Industries and Others* specifically involved auditors, the introduction of 'class actions' (or 'representative actions') as a means of litigation in the UK clearly suggests that it might no longer be necessary for aggrieved shareholders (and others?) to bring *individual* actions against auditors. This form of lawsuit permits aggrieved parties to combine in bringing a collective action, and as such represents a new and potent threat.

'The concept of a class action is perfectly sound in principle: it enables any class of persons who have suffered loss or damage attributable to one general cause, to combine for the purpose of bringing a joint action for their mutual benefit — usually involving the appointment of a "class trustee" to act on their behalf.

'Instances of its successful application are numerous: compensation following airline disasters attributable to manufacturing or servicing defect is an oft-quoted example; the damages payable to the victims of the massive *Equity Funding* fraud in 1973 were similarly settled by class action. Despite its obvious advantages of administrative efficiency and promptness of settlement, we have no equivalent principle in this country: witness, for example, the delay of a dozen or more years in achieving settlements of cases brought by victims of the thalidomide drug.

'Perhaps the closest we have come to the idea of a class action was the judgement of Lord Denning in the Hartley Baird case *(Wallersteiner v. Moir)* a few years ago, in permitting the considerable costs incurred by Mr. Moir in bringing this successful action to be reimbursed out of corporate resources — on the ground that the shareholders, as a class, had benefited from his endeavours.

'In February of this year, in what appears to be an even more explicit example of a UK class action, the Prudential Assurance Company has succeeded, on behalf of all shareholders in Newman Industries, in winning heavy damages against two of the latter company's directors for circularising information which was held to be "tricky and misleading". But the full implication for UK case law of the decision has still to be analysed.

'The practice of charging fees on a "contingency" basis, however, is wholly unprofessional and is understandably prohibited by the Law Society in this country. Legal fees in the UK, like the fees of most professionals, are based on the time, skill and level of responsibility required for the task undertaken, whereas in the US it is also permitted to charge a straight percentage of the damages awarded in cases of civil litigation.

'The potential consequences of this degree of licence are as obvious as they are horrendous. A lawyer bringing an action on behalf of a client has nothing to lose (and everything to gain) by pitching the claim as high as his mercenary imagination will stretch, for the sky is truly the limit. The vicious combination of class actions and contingency fees thus transforms every situation of corporate malpractice, even mismanagement, into a potential legal scenario:

(a) A skilled legal practitioner acquires a few shares in a company whose poor performance has produced a degree of restlessness amongst its members.

(b) He abuses his rights as a member to inquire into various aspects of corporate decision-making over the past few years, perhaps resorting to payment of a few legitimate "commissions" *en route* in return for exploitable information.

(c) He "concludes" that (i) the officers have been grossly negligent in the performance of certain of their duties; (ii) the accounts which they and the audit committee have passed for presentation to members have been materially misleading; (iii) the auditors have failed in their reporting duties to draw attention to the foregoing matters in their report; and (iv) a *prima facie* case therefore exists against all those previously cited.

(d) He invites the shareholders to form themselves into an aggrieved class, and to appoint him as the class trustee for the purposes of the action. They, like he, have little to lose, since the game is played according to the rule of "no victory, no fee"!

'Faced with vindictive damages it is not surprising that accounting firms are so often forced, for economic reasons, to defend themselves in court. What *is* surprising, however, is the number of occasions on which extravagant charges actually result in awards of damages of comparable amount.

'Such an arrangement, unlike that in the UK, renders collusion between judge and litigating advocate an obvious temptation. One would like, of course, to declare that corruption at that level is unthinkable — even in the US! — but unfortunately such sanguine assessments have borne more than their share of disillusionment in the decade just past.

'Without so much as a hint of complacency, it is fair to observe that, thanks to foundations which were consciously laid in this realm several centuries before out transatlantic brethren were chasing buffaloes and Red Indians across the plains, our legal system does not allow of such flamboyant abuse; professional self-protection based on any other supposition is unwarranted and is more, rather than less, likely to provide actual substance to these present fears!'

## Third Party Liability — Through the Post

A recent issue of *True and Fair* puts a spotlight on a highly unwelcome development in the realm of potential liability. A number of auditors have recently received letters from potential investors who are about to acquire substantial interests in companies whose accounts have been audited by those to whom the letters are addressed. These letters usually contain statements along the following lines:

(a) We are writing to advise you that we are contemplating making a substantial investment in XYZ Limited, of which we understand you are the auditor.

(b) We have not commissioned an independent report relating to the financial position of XYZ Limited.

(c) We shall place material reliance upon the audited accounts of XYZ Limited when making a decision as to whether or not to proceed with such an investment.

The import of such letters obviously suggests a wider accountability on the part of the auditor than is presently envisaged under the statutes, and is designed to exploit the uncertain nature of the common law in the direction of third party liability. The APC suggests that a formal reply to such letters should be made, in which it is clearly pointed out that accounts prepared and audited under the Companies Acts are not designed for use in an investment context, and that while they will undoubtedly contain useful information for such a purpose, they are no effective substitute for a specially commissioned acquisition or investigation report. Reference should also be made to the fact that published accounts do not convey the company's *current* financial situation, and they will, in any case, have incorporated management estimates acceptable to the auditor in the context of the company's overall financial position, but which may turn out subsequently to be significantly different.

Whether or not such a rebuttal of the validity of stewardship accounts being used for purposes of making investment decisions is effective, is a matter which only the courts can decide. Counsel's opinion (1966) following the famous *Hedley Byrne* decision (1963) maintained that no third party liability would attach to auditors if the accounts they have audited under the Companies Acts are used, without their knowledge or consent, by outsiders in an investment context. But this opinion was given prior to the Companies Act 1967 requirement that *all* companies should publish their accounts as a matter of public record, thereby effectively putting auditors on notice that the accounts could be examined by anyone, and for any purpose — investment decisions not excluded.

Nevertheless, it is likely that the reply suggested by the APC will prove legally effective, simply because it would clearly be unwise, and grossly incautious, for anyone to rely upon conventional audited accounts *exclusively* in reaching an investment decision. What is always risky, of course, is the possibility that any reliance on the audited statements may be regarded as *reasonable*, such reliance having featured within the context of a wider investigation, orientated towards investment. In such a case any loss traceable to the negligence of the auditor could not easily be defended on the grounds previously suggested. Even the APC freely admits that "statutory accounts contain much information of use to a potential investor" — to quote *True and Fair*.

## The 'Jeb Fasteners' and 'Twomax' Decisions

Growing fears over the past dozen years or so that auditors liability, if tested in court, would now prove to be virtually open-ended have recently been all but confirmed.

31

In 1981 in the widely reported case of *Jeb Fasteners Ltd. v. Marks, Bloom & Co.*, the 'proximity' or 'neighbourhood' principle was revised to render an auditor legally liable for the financial loss of an investor who *reasonably* relied on the auditor's negligent work in reaching the investment decision.

So far as the test of 'reasonableness' was concerned, it was held that the greater the period which elapsed between the issue of the negligently audited statements and the reliance upon it by the investor, the less reasonable would such reliance be.

The effect of this decision was to set aside such previously pertinent considerations (suggested by Counsel in 1966, following the *Hedley Byrne* decision) as, for example, whether the auditor *knew* that the financial statements, etc., were to be relied upon by the party who suffered the loss; and whether such reliance took place in the *specific context* in which the statements were prepared — thus separating for this purpose the investment and the stewardship contexts respectively.

It now seems that liability rests almost entirely on whether the reliance which led to the loss falls within this new view of reasonableness: indeed, in the *Jeb Fasteners* case, the fact that the defendant auditors did not know that the plaintiffs existed, let alone that their investment decision was alleged to have been based on the financial statements, had no bearing on the final judgement.

It so happens that the auditors were not in fact required to recompense the plaintiffs, but this part of the judgement was based on the judge's view that the decision to acquire the company concerned was reached independently of the negligently audited financial statements; and this conclusion was not reversed on appeal. What matters to the profession, however, is the revision of the proximity principle, which now clearly contends that it is reasonable for potential investors to rely on audited financial statements (prepared in a stewardship context) for the purpose of reaching an investment decision, irrespective of whether the auditor is aware of such reliance.

This principle has been further strengthened in a Scottish decision by Lord Stewart (*Twomax Ltd. & Goode v. Dickson, McFarlane & Robinson, March 1982*) in a case also involving the decision to acquire shares, based on negligently audited financial statements. Lord Stewart cited and quoted with evident enthusiasm the *Jeb Fasteners* judgement, and awarded damages of some £65,000, plus costs, against the auditors.

The legal liability of auditors to third parties has clearly reached new frontiers.


## Fraud Detection

A recent issue of the *Accounting and Auditing Newsletter* of Deloitte, Haskins & Sells included a useful reminder of the responsibilities of auditors in the realm of fraud detection, as follows.

The possibility of fraud occurring is always real but, in times of economic depression when company profits are squeezed and interest rates and inflation rates are high, fraud becomes even more likely. One recent example was the fraud disclosed in the press at the end of April in which contractors employed by the CEGB falsely claimed sums totalling £250,000 for power station maintenance work that was never carried out. In that particular case, both the contractors and their employees directly benefited from the additional false claims. Fraud of this nature is increasingly likely when wages fail to keep pace with rising prices.

The two main areas of fraud that auditors should be alert for during their work are:

(a) the manipulating of the financial statements by members of management, either to meet business and financial expectations or to obtain indirect personal gain (including staying in a job);

(b) the abstracting of assets (primarily cash) by either members of management or employees for personal gain.

When auditors fulfil audit and other engagements, they should consider the possibility that fraud may have been perpetrated for either or both of the reasons stated above. To help with this task, they should ask certain key questions. A list of appropriate (but not exhaustive) questions is set out below:

(a) Manipulation of the financial statements. A 'yes' answer to any of the following questions indicates an increased risk that the financial statements may have been manipulated:
    (i)    Have the company's operations deteriorated recently?
    (ii)   Do present business conditions indicate potential future difficulties for the company?
    (iii)  Is the company likely to have difficulty in meeting its financial obligations as they become due?
    (iv)  Is there an intention either to liquidate or to curtail significantly the scale of operations?
    (v)   Does the company propose to raise substantial additional finance in the near future?
    (vi)  Is there likely to be a contest for control of the company in the near future?
    (vii) Is there likely to be a change of control of the company in the near future?
    (viii) Is more than the usual significance likely to be attached to the financial statements?
(b) Abstraction of assets. Auditors should consider the following:
    (i)    Are excessive discretionary powers granted either to new employees or to employees of comparatively low calibre?
    (ii)   Are wage levels below the average for either the locality or the industry?
    (iii)  Is there unexplained extravagance by any employees (especially those who are in key positions and have custody of assets)?
    (iv)  Does any employee refuse to take his due holiday (which may be because he wishes to avoid having his duties subjected to the independent scrutiny of a relief employee)?
    (v)   Are any employees either excessively uncooperative or antagonistic towards the auditors or are they excessively cooperative?
    (vi)  Does a single individual unaccountably dominate the activities of any department, branch or activity?
    (vii) Are accounting records consistently written up a long time after the transactions they record have taken place?
    (viii) Are filing systems such that, for no apparent reason, documents are difficult to retrieve?

A positive answer to any of these questions does not necessarily mean that fraud is taking place. However, a positive answer does indicate that auditors need to consider carrying out further audit tests to overcome the inherent risks. The decision to extend tests will depend upon the combination of various factors and will require consultation between the partner, the manager and the senior responsible for the engagement.

# 5 Audit Management (Including Audit Report Checklist)

*If auditing practices are to provide the best possible service to their clients, it is important that their approach to audit work should be properly planned and managed. 'Audit Management', as it is often termed, has become a popular examination topic in recent sittings and these notes explain the importance of audit planning; the institution of quality control procedures; standardisation of audit techniques; and review procedures. This section should be studied in conjunction with that on the 'Auditing Standards' issued by the Auditing Practices Committee, dealt with in Chapter 2.*

From time to time questions appear in examinations on problems of controlling the audit, from the point of view of the auditing firm itself.

The effective management of the audit involves three objectives:

(a) ensuring that the auditing practice operates profitably;
(b) providing a high level of service to clients; and
(c) taking all reasonable steps towards avoiding liability.

These objectives are usually achieved in two ways:

(a) by effective audit planning; and
(b) instituting procedures for quality control.

Each of these areas may be further expanded.

## Audit Planning

Planning the audit, especially a large audit, involves close liaison with the client company's financial director and his staff. As much of the work as possible should be completed at the interim stage, leaving the final audit clear for such matters as verification of assets and liabilities, the final review of the accounts and checking that disclosure requirements have been complied with.

Where joint audits are undertaken, planning the allocation of work between the two firms ought to take place several months before it is due to be performed. Similarly, the external auditors should be in close touch with the internal audit staff in order to avoid unnecessary overlap of work and at the same time to ensure that, between them, all detailed audit procedures are satisfactorily completed.

Most client companies have a detailed programme of work leading up to the final preparation of their annual accounts, and the auditor should be provided with the details of this programme for his own planning purposes. This is especially useful in connection with routine matters such as:

(a) stock verification;
(b) cash count;
(c) securities count;
(d) debtor circularisation.

By careful planning at all stages of the audit, the auditing firm can ensure, as far as possible, *the availability of the right number of each grade of staff required on the audit team, at every stage of the audit.*

**Quality Control Procedures**

*Standardisation of Documentation*

The detailed content of all audit files should, as far as possible, be pre-determined, and their completion ensured by the use of standard indices.

The permanent file, for example, will include details of:

(a) history and nature of business;
(b) copies of memorandum and articles;
(c) sets of previous accounts for 2/3 years;
(d) extracts of essential contents of documents such as long-term contracts; leases; insurance policies; title deeds;
(e) extracts from previous years' accounts indicating trend of business; divisional results; key ratios, etc;
(f) copy of the original letter of engagement and any amendments thereto.

It is even more important that the current audit file should be complete and, for the duration of the audit in question, certain documents of a permanent nature (e.g. Internal Control Questionnaire) will be transferred to the current file.

The standard contents of the current file (including documents effectively in use for longer than one audit period) should be incorporated in the standard index, and the following documents will obviously be included:

(a) current draft accounts and supporting schedules;
(b) detailed audit programme;
(c) internal control questionnaire (ICQ);
(d) internal control evaluation (ICE);
(e) flow diagrams;
(f) letters of weakness (more than one may be issued during the audit);
(g) letter of representation;
(h) standard confirmations from:
   bank, re all account balances and securities held for safe custody;
   finance companies and others re loans/mortgages;
   warehouse/agents, for goods held at docks awaiting clearnace or for re-export; goods held by others on a sale or return basis; goods held by consignees;
   members of staff for loans;
   foreign agents and associated firms, for client assets held abroad;
   circularisation of debtors;
(i) checklists;
   Companies Act requirements — including 1981 Act formats, details of directors' emoluments, loans to officers, quasi-loans, contracts and other transactions with directors (Companies Act 1980), and Section 12 (1976) on proper accounting records;
   SSAPs (noting particularly the date from which operative);
   Stock Exchange requirements for listed companies;
   Contents of Directors' Report;
   Requirements under other statutes and regulations, e.g. Building Societies, Friendly Societies, solicitors, etc.
(j) special checklist for the audit report, as follows:

| | Yes | No | Not Applicable |
|---|---|---|---|

Technical content

(i) Have all the explanations and information necessary for the purposes of the audit been obtained — with particular reference to certificates and confirmations from third parties and auditors and directors of subsidiaries?

(ii) Have proper accounting records been kept and proper returns received from any branches not visited?

(iii) Are the accounts in agreement with the records and returns?

(iv) Do the accounts give a true view of the result for the year and the state of affairs at the year-end?

(v) Do the accounts give not only a *true* but also a *fair* view?

(vi) Do the accounts comply with the requirements of the Companies Acts 1948 to 1981?

(vii) Are details of the following items included in the audit report to the extent that they are not properly disclosed in the accounts?

> directors' emoluments, pensions, and compensation for loss of office?
> loans and quasi-loans to officers?
> material contracts and other transactions with directors covered by disclosure requirements of the Companies Act 1980.
> chairman's emoluments?
> emoluments of highest paid director (other than chairman)?
> directors' emoluments waived?
> the number of directors and employees whose emoluments fall within specified statutory bands?

(viii) Where appropriate, do the group accounts show a true and fair view of the group position and comply with the requirements of the Companies Acts 1948 to 1981?

(ix) Where appropriate, does the audit report include qualifications contained in the reports of subsidiary audit firms to the extent that the qualifications are material in the context of the group accounts as whole?

(x) Have questionnaires, sent to subsidiary auditors, been duly completed and returned to our satisfaction?

(xi) Does the audit report refer, in appropriate terms, to all significant departures from Accounting Standards?

(xii) Does the audit report include a reference to the statement of source and application of funds (SSAP 10), where appropriate?

36

| | Yes | No | Not Applicable |
|---|---|---|---|
| (xiii) Does the audit report refer in appropriate terms to supplementary information included in the accounts pursuant to the requirements of SSAP 16 on Current Cost Accounting? | | | |
| (xiv) Have the accounts been approved and signed by the directors *before* the audit report is signed? | | | |
| (xv) Have all outstanding queries been satisfactorily resolved? | | | |
| (xvi) Have we, in the conduct of our audit and the drafting of our report, complied with the requirements of Auditing Standards 1 to 3? | | | |
| (xvii) Have we examined the directors' report in pursuance to Section 15 (1981), and if so are we satisfied that it is consistent with the financial statements? | | | |
| (xviii) If the answer to the previous question is 'no', have we referred to the inconsistency in our report, as required? | | | |
| (xix) If our report is qualified, and a dividend has been declared, have we stated whether our qualification is material for purposes of ascertaining the legitimacy of the dividend? | | | |

Possible clerical errors

(i)  Does the audit report refer to the correct accounting reference date and period?

(ii) Does the report refer correctly to the 'profit' or 'loss' for the period? (It may be preferable to refer to 'results', especially where a 'profit' is shown *before* tax and extraordinary items, and a 'loss' arises *after* one or both of these.)

(iii) Are the references in the report to page numbers in the accounts correct?

(iv) Is the audit report correctly addressed?

(v) Has a partner, not in any way involved with the audit in question,
 – independently read the draft auditor's report and approved its technical content and the suitability of the wording relating to any departures from the clean 'short-form' report?
 – reviewed the above checklist?

## Standardisation of Audit Techniques

The standardisation of documentation is only a partial contribution towards esablishment and maintenance of quality control. It is most important that all audit staff should be familiar with the use of the audit techniques as practised by the firm, and for this purpose it is usual for extensive 'in house' training programmes to be arranged for all levels of staff, employing formal instruction as well as case study techniques, as appropriate. The contents of these programmes will have specific application to:

(a)  use of standard symbols in flow charting techniques;

(b)  guidelines governing the use of statistical sampling techniques (e.g. where this method may or may not be appropriate), and the use of sampling procedures in general;

(c)  procedures for observation of physical stocktaking;

(d)  action to be taken on discovery of internal control weaknesses and/or compensating controls;

(e)  increasing dependence upon computer processing by clients;

(f)  implications of new accounting, auditing and legal developments.

*Review of Quality Control*

The maintenance of auditing standards requires constant vigilance and many firms appoint partners to a committee (sometimes referred to as 'Post-Audit Review' committee).

It is the responsibility of this committee:

(a)  to determine the level of audit testing required in particular circumstances;

(b)  to determine the appropriate techniques to be used by staff;

(c)  to disseminate up-to-date information to staff at all appropriate levels;

(d)  to organise suitable training courses, the content of which should be geared to the level of staff attending;

(e)  to constantly monitor standards operating in every office which carries the firm's name. Staff suggestions based on field tests and general feedback should be taken fully into account in this connection.

Some major international firms have taken this review a degree further by arranging unexpected visits to branch offices in any part of the world with a view to inspecting accounts/working paper files/audit reports, etc., as a means of assessing the extent to which the local office is consistently applying the firm's predetermined standards.

The ultimate in such reviews arises where one major firm invites a rival firm to undertake a review of its standards and methods on a completely independent basis. In the United States, the Securities and Exchange Commission has recently requisitioned such a review in the case of one major firm and it is the intention of the SEC that this form of review, known as a 'peer review', should operate more widely.

# 6 Amounts Derived from Preceding Financial Statements

*Although the page numbers referred to at the commencement of all audit reports (indicating the financial statements subjected to audit) include prior period comparatives, the audit opinion never makes reference to these. By contrast, auditors in the USA always express their opinion on the statements for both financial periods. Do auditors take full responsibility for the prior period comparatives shown? Would such responsibility be different (i.e. greater or less) if another firm had audited them? In October 1981 the APC issued the following draft Guideline on this problematic area of responsibility. A full Guideline was issued in November 1982, but is not significantly different from the draft.*

## Introduction

1. Consideration of the financial statements of the preceding period is necessary in the audit of the current period's financial statements in relation to the following three aspects, namely:

   (a) the opening position: obtaining satisfaction that those amounts which have a direct effect on the current period's results or closing position have been properly brought forward;
   (b) accounting policies: determining whether the accounting policies adopted for the current period are consistent with those of the previous period;
   (c) corresponding amounts: determining that the corresponding amounts, also referred to as comparative figures, are properly shown in the current period's financial statements.

2. Financial statements of companies incorporated under the provisions of the Companies Acts are required to disclose corresponding amounts 'at the end of the immediately preceding financial year for all items in the balance sheet' and 'for the immediately preceding financial year for all items shown in the profit and loss account'. In other cases, financial statements usually contain corresponding amounts as a matter of good practice. Their purpose, unless stated otherwise, is to complement the amounts relating to the current period and not to re-present the complete financial statements for the preceding period.

3. If the auditor himself has issued an unqualified report on the preceding period's financial statements and his audit of the current period has not revealed any matters which cast doubts on those financial statements, he should not need to extend his audit procedures beyond:

   (a) satisfying himself that amounts have been correctly brought forward and incorporated in the accounting records of the current period, and
   (b) ensuring that they are properly classified and disclosed as corresponding amounts.

If he is satisfied with the results of these procedures, it should not be necessary for him to make any reference to amounts taken from the preceding period's financial statements in his report on the current period's financial statements.

4. Additional considerations may apply in any of the following circumstances:

   (a) the opening position and corresponding amounts are derived from financial statements which have been audited by another auditor or are unaudited;
   (b) the audit report on the financial statements of the preceding period was qualified;
   (c) the corresponding amounts have been re-stated, or a re-statement is justified but has not been made.

## Preceding Period Audited by Another Auditor or Unaudited

5. The auditor will often be able to satisfy himself as regards the closing position shown by a balance sheet without specific reference to the opening position. He will, however, have to satisfy himself as to the opening position as disclosed by the preceding period's balance sheet in order to express an opinion on the current period's profit or loss and state of affairs. He will need also to ensure that there is consistency in accounting policies and classification of balances.

6. The work performed by the auditor to satisfy himself regarding the opening position may include any of the following:

(a) consultations with the client's management;
(b) review of the client's records, working papers and accounting and control procedures for the preceding period, so far as they affect the opening position;
(c) audit work on the current period, which will frequently provide some evidence regarding opening balances;
(d) consultations with the previous auditor, if any. Such consultations, which would be similar to those undertaken by primary auditors in relation to group accounts, may involve discussions and examination of a predecessor's audit files, working papers and any relevant management letters.

The emphasis to be placed on each of the above will depend upon the circumstances, and will also vary according to the impact on the current period's results of possible errors in the preceding period's balance sheet. A materially incorrect stock figure, for instance, will normally have a serious effect on the results shown for the current period.

7. Under normal circumstances the auditor will be able to satisfy himself as to the opening position by performing the work set out in para 6. If he is not able to satisfy himself in any material respect he will need to qualify his report for the possible effect on the financial statements. A form of report is set out below which might be suitable where the preceding period's audit report was unqualified, and the area of difficulty was material but not fundamental.

AUDITORS' REPORT TO THE MEMBERS OF . . .
We have audited the financial statements on pages . . . to . . ., which have been prepared under the historical cost convention. Our audit was conducted in accordance with approved Auditing Standards, except that the scope of our work was limited by the matter referred to below.

The financial statements for last year were reported upon by other auditors. The company's accounting records are such that it was not possible for us to carry out the auditing procedures necessary to obtain our own assurance in relation to the opening financial position as regards certain stock and work in progress, appearing in the preceding period's financial statements at £. . . Any adjustment to this figure would have a consequential effect on the profit for the current year.

In our opinion the balance sheet gives a true and fair view of the state of the company's affairs at 31 December 19.. and, subject to the effect of any adjustment which might have been necessary in respect of the foregoing, the financial statements give a true and fair view of the profit and source and application of funds for the year then ended, and comply with the Companies Acts 1948 to 1981.

If the area of difficulty was fundamental then the auditor would need to consider whether to disclaim an opinion on the profit and source and application of funds.

## Preceding Period's Qualifications

8. If the audit report on the preceding period's financial statements was qualified, but the matter giving rise to the qualification has been satisfactorily resolved and dealt with in the financial statements, then normally no reference need be made in the current period's audit report. If, however, the matter which gave rise to the qualification remains unresolved and affects the current period's financial statements, the audit report should be qualified. In such a case, the notes to the financial statements should adequately disclose the circumstances surrounding the qualification. The

auditor may consider it advisable to refer to the previous qualification so as to make it clear that the matter giving rise to the qualification did not arise in the current period. A form of report which might be suitable is set out below:

AUDITORS' REPORT TO THE MEMBERS OF . . .

We have audited the financial statements on pages . . . to . . . in accordance with approved Auditing Standards.

As indicated in note . . . to the financial statements, debtors include an amount of £ . . which is subject to litigation but against which no provision has been made as the directors state that they have no reason to suppose that the amount will not be recovered in full. We qualified our audit report on the financial statements at 31 December 19.. (date of preceding financial statements) with regard to this same uncertainty.

Subject to the adjustment, if any, that may be required when the litigation is settled, in our opinion the financial statements, which have been prepared under the historical cost convention, give a true and fair view of the state of the company's affairs at 31 December 19.. and of the profit and source and application of funds for the year then ended and comply with the Companies Acts 1948 to 1981.

9. If the audit report on the preceding period's financial statements was qualified, for example by a disclaimer on the profit and loss account because of uncertainty over the opening balances but an unqualified opinion was given on the balance sheet, it will usually be necessary to refer to that fact in the current period's audit report. Such a reference would put the reader on notice that the corresponding amounts may be incorrectly stated.

Since no qualification of the opinion on the current period's figures is implied that is best done as an 'emphasis of matter'. An additional paragraph which might be suitable for inclusion in the audit report is set out below:

'The corresponding amounts in the current period's financial statements are derived from the financial statements for the year ended 31 December 19.. (date of previous financial statements). In our report on those financial statements we stated that we were unable to express an opinion on the profit and source and application of funds for the year ended on that date because we were unable to substantiate the amount of stock at 1 January 19.. (preceding year). However, the above matter does not affect the view which we express below on the current period's financial statements.

**Restatement of Corresponding Amounts**

10. In certain situations, such as changes in accounting policies or corrections of fundamental errors, it is necessary for the corresponding amounts to be restated in the manner required by Statement of Standard Accounting Practice No. 6. Restatement of corresponding amounts may also be desirable in other circumstances, for example where there have been reclassifications in the current period.

11. If the auditor is satisfied that the corresponding amounts have been correctly restated and described in the financial statements it will not normally be necessary for him to make any reference thereto in his report. If the auditor does not concur with a restatement, or if in his opinion a restatement is necessary but has not been made, he should consider qualifying his report.

# 7 Contemporary Banking Problems

*The difficulties experienced by the 'fringe' or 'secondary' banking sector in the seventies are now legion and the repercussions will be felt for many years. The brief note which follows suggests the audit considerations which should be borne in mind when reviewing the financial strength of this type of bank in the future.*

*Note:* Audit problems in connection with specialised companies and institutions fall within the published syllabus. Most basic audit considerations will be obvious from an examination of the accounts of such institutions; however, examiners now appear to require more than a superficial description of audit procedures, and this note therefore describes the more problematic considerations which auditors should bear in mind when reviewing accounts of companies in the banking sector.

## Introduction and Background — the Early Seventies

The difficulties encountered by the fringe banking sector in recent years are now widely known, and a number of lessons have now, hopefully, been learnt. In essence, the disasters were attributable to the banks' speculative involvement with property development companies to whom vast amounts of finance were allocated, on the ill-conceived basis that property prices would continue to spiral upwards indefinitely.

Until a property development is complete no income is received, and consequently many of the banks who lent on the strength of future prospects were obliged to 'roll up' their interest charges (i.e. compound them and add them to the capital), even though they were themselves paying interest rates on the money market of as high as 15% to 22%.

When the upward trend in property prices reached its peak in 1974 and began to move into reverse, a large number of speculative development projects came to an immediate halt, often bringing bankruptcy to the building contractors involved; thus the waiting game began and in the unsettled state of the property market even the giants were at a loss as to the valuation of their portfolio in the annual accounts — hence the proliferation of qualifications in the auditors' reports.

The above chain of events inevitably led to 'lifeboat' operations by the clearing banks under the auspices of the bank of England. Now that much of the dust has settled, revealing a drastically pruned property sector and fringe banking fraternity, the 'senior citizens' of the City establishments are concerned to avoid a similar catastrophe in the eighties.

The Bank of England, in particular, has tightened its supervisory role and is thus aiding the health of the banking industry as a whole. The Bank of England currently seeks a good deal of detailed information from individual banking institutions; this is sought once a year from the clearers, but more frequently from the smaller banks. The range of questions being asked is wide, and accords closely with the kind of questions which the banks' auditors should be asking. It is therefore worth examining some of the enquiries in detail:

(a) When looking at a bank's profit and loss account it is important to discover precisely what proportions of the bank's profits are derived from the hard core of sustainable business, and how much from sources of income which, if not speculative, are at least uncertain. For example, the auditor should examine the proportions of income derived from the following three sources:

     (i)   net interest margins between lending and borrowing.

     (ii)  dealing profits derived from the bank's investment portfolio;

     (iii) fees and commissions received and receivable.

(b) Although auditing a prior period, auditors should discuss current problems with the bank's management to discover whether profits are being made in the current trading period.

(c) Enquiries should be made as to whether such projected profits take into account suspended interest 'rolled up', realistic bad debt provisions, and any other decline in the realisable value of assets.

(d) The auditors should enquire when such provisions were last reviewed by the bank's own management and how frequently such reviews are made.

Enquiries along these lines would indicate some of the background detail of a bank's trading account, and establish the trend of its business; such enquiries would also show whether the bank is essentially profitable or is relying upon dealing or windfall profits, and therefore at risk.


## Normal or Abnormal?

Given the versatility which banking institutions now require in order to remain viable, it is not always a simple matter to distinguish between normal and abnormal events. For example, in relation to interest received and paid, the following questions are relevant:

(a) Are net interest margins positive, particularly in relation to the funding of the bank's own fixed assets the acquisition of which may require funding at current rates of interest?

(b) How much interest receivable is being suspended, *and* on what proportion of the total loan portfolio?

In relation to questions such as these there is little collective experience as to what should be regarded as normal or abnormal respectively.

With high interest rates, many bank customers may experience cash flow difficulties in meeting their interest payments. Banks may be tempted in the circumstances to arrange 'refinancing' of customer debts, thus creating a further interest charge. Such arrangements may appear to be lucrative for the banks, but they remain highly speculative and may be merely serving to delay the impact of real financial difficulties. This is the 'micro' reflection of what is increasingly problematic on the 'macro' and international levels.


## Further Enquiries

Further enquiries should be aimed at establishing:

(a) The areas in which a bank is dealing, e.g.

     (i)   investments;

     (ii)  certificates of deposit;

     (iii) foreign exchange;

     (iv) commodities;

     (v)   land and property.

(b) The fee-earning activities of the bank, for example in respect of:

     (i)   loan commitments;

     (ii)  bill acceptances;

     (iii) portfolio management;

     (iv) corporate advisory work.

## Conclusion

The insight into the strength of the institution being audited, which the above approach is bound to give, will prove to be invaluable in assessing its viability. A thorough investigation along these lines will also provide indications of great benefit to management, particularly in alerting the latter to the danger signals which may be thrown up by their own management accounts — before it is too late to take remedial action.

# 8  The Audit of Building Societies

*Recent years have seen the collapse of a number of building societies, with or without a fraudulent ingredient. The two most recent collapses were the Wakefield and Grays, which have a good deal in common. A brief analysis of Grays may therefore be instructive and is included later in this chapter. The fraud, which resulted in a loss of over £7 million at latest estimate, contained a fair amount of sensational matter. It lasted for over 50 years and was brought to a conclusion by the suicide of the Chairman and Secretary of the Society, Mr. Harold Jaggard, at the age of 79.*

**Legal Requirements**

The governing legislation is the Building Societies Act 1962, and it will be seen from the following extracts that there are strong similarities between Building Societies and Companies legislation.

*Section 87*

(a) The auditors of a building society shall make a report to the members on the accounts examined by them, and on every balance sheet and every revenue and appropriation account laid before the society at the annual general meeting during their tenure of office.

(b) The auditors' report shall be read before the building society at the annual general meeting and shall be open to inspection by any member.

(c) The report shall state whether the balance sheet and revenue and appropriation account are properly drawn up in accordance with the requirements of this Act and the regulations made thereunder and whether, in the opinion of the auditors, they give a true and fair view:
  (i)  in the case of the balance sheet, of the state of the building society's affairs as at the end of its financial year; and
  (ii)  in the case of the revenue and appropriation account of the income and expenditure of the building society for its financial year.

(d) It shall be the duty of the auditors of a building society in preparing this report under this section to carry out such investigations as will enable them to form an opinion as to the following matter, that is to say;
  (i)  whether the society has kept proper books of account and proper records of the matters referred to in Section 27 of this Act;
  (ii)  whether the society has maintained a satisfactory system of control over its transactions and records; and
  (iii)  whether the balance sheet and revenue and appropriation account are in agreement with the books of account and records of the society;
  and if the auditors are of the opinion that the society has failed to keep proper books of account or proper records of the matters referred to in subsection 1 of Section 27 of this Act, or to maintain a satisfactory system of control over its transactions and records, or if the balance sheet and revenue and appropriation account are not in agreement with the books of account and records of the society, the auditors shall state that fact in their report.

(e) Every auditor of a building society:
  (i)  shall have a right of access at all times to the books, accounts, records and vouchers of the society and to all other documents relating to its affairs including the deeds relating to property mortgaged to the society; and

     (ii)  shall be entitled to require from the officers of the society such information and explanations as he thinks necessary for the performance of the duties of the auditors.

(f) If the auditors fail to obtain all the information and explanations which, to the best of their knowledge and belief, are necessary for the purposes of their audit, they shall state that fact in their report.

(g) The auditors of a building society shall be entitled:
    (i)  to attend any general meeting of the society and to receive all notices of and other communications relating to any general meeting which any member of the building society is entitled to receive; and
    (ii)  to be heard at any meeting which they attend on any part of the business of the meeting which concerns them as auditors.

*Section 91*

(a) The auditors of a building society shall make a report on the annual return which shall be annexed to the annual return made to the Chief Registrar of Friendly Societies.

(b) Regulations under Section 86 of this Act may provide that the auditors of a building society shall not be required in their report on the annual return to deal with such of the matters to be contained in the annual return as may be prescribed by the regulations for the purposes of this subsection.

(c) The auditors' report on the annual return shall (without prejudice to any provision of this Act requiring any other information to be contained therein) contain statements as to the following matters, that is to say:
    (i)  whether in their opinion the annual return is properly drawn up in accordance with the requirements of the Act and regulations made thereunder;
    (ii)  whether the annual return gives a true and fair view of the matters to which it is to be addressed (other than those which the auditors are by virtue of regulations made in pursuance of the last preceding subsection, not required to deal); and
    (iii)  whether the annual return is in agreement with the books of account and records of the society.

**The Grays Building Society Fraud**

*Cash Receipts and Payments*

As a background to analysing the Grays fraud it is necessary to note that the chief sources of building society receipts by cash and cheque are:

(a) deposits received;
(b) mortgage repayments, comprising
    (i)  capital, and
    (ii)  interest;
(c) mortgage redemptions (final).

The following are the major payments:

(a) interest on deposits;
(b) mortgage advances to vendors or their solicitors;
(c) payments to the building society's own solicitors (fees) and insurance premiums.

*The Nature of the Grays Fraud*

The D.o.T. report on Grays noted that the Chairman was
(a) misappropriating cash received,
(b) teeming and lading to cover up the deficiency,

(c) 'plugging the gap' by misallocating mortgage redemption cheques which, by their nature, usually comprise substantial amounts.

The Grays fraud was based on the simple principle that a certain ratio of liquidity was needed on a day-to-day basis and that other sums, over and above this ratio, were therefore susceptible to misappropriation. This principle applies in banks — there is little chance that under normal circumstances all depositors would wish to draw out their money on one day. The Chairman of Grays simply ensured that the Society's predictable cash requirements were always available. We now know what he did with the remainder, although the exact nature of his personal expenditure has not been established. He was a heavy gambler, and there were rumours of other 'extra-mural activities' — but we need not go into this here.

*The Cover-Up*

He was able to cover up the fraud:

   (a) By making the book entries (over which he had complete control) appear to reflect the actual transactions, i.e. as if the cash was present in the Society's account.

   (b) By controlling his co-directors, to whom Board Minutes were never circulated, and who clearly had little conception of the nature of their own statutory duties. They always 'rubber stamped' mortgage redemptions, but they never checked that the payments had actually been received and banked.

   (c) By hiring staff who were incapable of appreciating what he was doing or how his position in the society would naturally allow the exercise of a free hand, especially in relation to the manipulation of cash assets and supporting records.

   (d) By maintaining a handwritten recording system despite the fact that the Society's assets approached £10 million.

   (e) By effectively controlling the audit function.

*The Audit*

   (a) Tests carried out by the Grays' auditors were always carried out in an identical sequence. The Society's records were therefore presented to the auditors in the same sequence, and this enabled the Chairman to alter records after audit inspection. Incidentally, figures were always presented to the auditors in pencil, and as a result of subsequent alterations crosscasts *appeared* to agree but in fact did not.

   (b) The audit staff were clearly incompetent to understand the purpose of their tests. They were conducted mechanically, each stage of the audit being pursued in isolation from all other stages. The audit staff appear to have acted under the Chairman's control, and it was subsequently discovered that many of the tests laid down were never performed.

   (c) The partner responsible for the audit clearly did not know what was actually going on. For example, he did not know that

      (i)   all incoming mail was opened by the Chairman personally,

      (ii)  mortgage redemption cheques were always handed to the Chairman personally,

      (iii) the year-end summaries contained post-audit erasures and did not crosscast.

   (d) The audit partner did know that cash was not banked daily but, in his view, overcame this weakness by occasionally counting the cash. Unfortunately, however, such cash counts were never conducted on a surprise basis.

*Summary of the Grays Situation*

   (a) The accounting procedures were never subjected to review.

   (b) Internal control procedures as a whole were never subjected to review, either by the Board or by the auditors.

   (c) Neither the Board nor the auditors had any real idea of the possibilities open to the Chairman, nor of his ability to override such controls as were purported to exist.

## Department of Trade Recommendations

The D.o.T. Inspectors recommend as follows:

(a) Strengthening the powers and procedures available to the Registrar of Building Societies concerning the review of Societies' operations and the effectiveness of their auditors.

(b) Provision by Building Society auditors of a more explicit and detailed report as part of the annual return.

(c) 'It is good practice for the auditors to meet the Board, or the appropriate Committee, at least once a year to discuss the accounts, the accounting procedures and the internal control.' It is recommended that the auditors should confirm in their report that this has been done.

(d) It is recommended that the ability and knowledge of Building Society directors in general should be enhanced, and that they should be required to resign and seek annual re-election upon reaching the age of 70 (as is the case under the Companies Acts).

(e) The law should be changed to ensure that the Chairman of a Building Society should not also act as Chief Executive.

(f) There should be at least two executive directors on every Building Society Board.

Finally, the Inspectors recommend that they should be able to apply to the Court for an order to compel witnesses to attend. The Grays' Inspectors were unable to compel certain witnesses (e.g. the bookmakers, whose cooperation would have been necessary to ascertain more accurately the personal expenditure of the Chairman) to answer their questions. Such a power exists, of course, under the Companies Act 1967, but this does not extend to building societies.

## Institute Guidelines

Some years ago the Institute of Chartered Accountants in England and Wales issued guidelines on the audit of Building Society accounts. The appropriate extracts are as follows:

### Limitations in the Rules

The rules and policy of the society may impose limitations as to:

(a) types of property which may be accepted as security;

(b) proportion of the value of the security which may be advanced;

(c) overall limit on the amount which may be advanced either per property, per borrower or over a stated period;

(d) types of additional security which may be accepted and any special conditions;

(e) the competent persons who are eligible to value properties;

(f) advances on properties in course of erection;

(g) rates of interest and repayment terms.

### Records of Advances

The records maintained by the society in respect of advances should include the following which are hereafter referred to as the 'advance records', irrespective of the form they may take in any particular society:

(a) offers of advances and by whom authorised;

(b) security for advances, survey report, solicitors' report on title, and status reports;

(c) name and address of borrower;

(d) terms;

(e) records of compliance with any conditions;

(f)  board approval;

(g)  acceptance or withdrawal of applications.

## The Auditors' Examination

The auditors have a statutory duty to carry out such investigations as will enable them to form an opinion whether the foregoing requirement has been complied with. Particular points to consider in examining the system include:

(a)  the procedure for checking deeds on receipt from the solicitors to see that they are complete in accordance with the 'advance records' , correctly executed and stamped;

(b)  the maintenance of a record showing the location of all the deeds and the dates of any changes in the location of any of them;

(c)  the procedure for ensuring that the deeds are received from the society's solicitors without undue delay; solicitors frequently need to submit documents to the Land Registry and as there is often a delay of some months at the Registry it is important that the society should have an established follow-up procedure, to ensure that the receipt of deeds from the solicitors is not delayed longer than is necessary for registration to be completed;

(d)  the authority required for any temporary release of deeds from their normal custody and proper control for their prompt return;

(e)  whether there is a continuous independent check (which some large societies maintain) of the deeds against the advance records or the borrowers' ledger accounts;

(f)  the necessity for satisfactory cross-reference between the advance records, the cash-book, the borrowers' ledger accounts and the deeds;

(g)  the procedure for release of deeds on redemption of a mortgage; on premature redemption the discharge of a mortgage will usually have to be completed by the society and passed, with the title deeds, to the society's solicitors some time before the redemption money is received and there should therefore be an established follow-up procedure.

## Examining the Deeds

When examining the deeds the auditors' purpose should be to ascertain whether:

(a)  the mortgage is in the name shown in the advance records, unless it is a 'transfer of equity' in which case the mortgage would be in the name of the original mortgagor while the name in the advance records should be that of the transferee in the new document of title;

(b)  there is a document of title to the property under mortgage and the society's solicitors have been satisfied as to the borrower's title:

(c)  the amount of the advance as stated in the mortgage deed is not less than that shown on the advance records;

(d)  the mortgage deed is stamped, properly signed and witnessed and is *prima facie* in order;

(e)  the property is adequately insured, the premium is paid up to date and the society's interest as mortgagee is endorsed on the insurance policy.

## Shares and Deposits

(a)  An indication is given below of matters which the auditors will need to consider when assessing the system and deciding what tests they should apply in order to satisfy themselves on the records of shares and deposits. An effective confirmation of balances is a most important safeguard and the auditors should either carry out or supervise the carrying out of a test confirmation at least once a year.

(b)  Shares may consist of subscription shares and paid-up shares; there are also term shares where the shareholder will not normally require repayment until after a specified period of years. Interest on shares or deposits may be credited to the account instead of being paid. The following should be covered by the society's system to ensure proper control:

(i)    responsible custody of unused share and deposit passbooks, receipt forms and share certificates;

(ii)   instructions to the staff as to the making of entries in passbooks, and the issue of receipts;

(iii)  withdrawal terms, notice, specimen signatures;

(iv)  authorisation of withdrawals by ledger department or against passbook;

(v)   records of deaths, marriages, powers of attorney and transmission of shares and deposits. Direct transfers from one account to another should not be permitted. Transfers should be entered in a journal so that all such entries may be verified;

(vi)  comparison of the balance shown in the passbook with that shown in the ledger account; this may be carried out continuously by retaining passbooks for comparison before return or by periodical circularisation of depositors or shareholders requesting them to send in their passbooks for the purpose. It is desirable that the Society's system should provide for special arrangements to deal with withdrawals from accounts where correspondence has been returned unanswered or trace has otherwise been lost of depositors or shareholders.

## Cash

The handling of cash is always accompanied by possibilities of error and misappropriation, concealed by 'teeming and lading', manipulation of dormant accounts and other devices. This problem is of special importance to auditors of building societies because of the large extent of the cash transactions, but it does not involve audit considerations which differ in principle from those encountered in many other businesses. In assessing the system and testing its effectiveness the auditors will need to apply rigorously their professional techniques. Discrepancies revealed by surprise cash accounts or by searching tests 'in depth' will call for exhaustive investigation.

## 'Window Dressing'

Auditors should examine transactions which have the effect of showing as on the balance sheet date a state of affairs (particularly the society's liquidity) which is materially better than it was during the year and shortly after. Items requiring particular attention are:

(a) large deposits received shortly before the year end and repaid shortly after;

(b) large mortgage repayments received shortly before the year end and re-advanced on the same property shortly after;

(c) unusual delay until after the year end in making payments in accordance with applications received for withdrawals of shares or deposits;

(d) an abnormal year end accumulation of commitments for advances followed by the making of the advances shortly after the year end;

(e) the significance of the items in bank reconciliation statements.

## Specimen Auditor's Report

The auditor's report must be addressed to the members of the Society. The matters on which the auditor must report are set out in Section 87. As is the case with all auditor's reports, it should clearly indicate those areas of the financial statements on which the auditor is reporting. It is usual to deal with this by stating the page numbers of the financial statements in the report. It is becoming more common for the statement of source and application of funds (often called the movement of funds statement) to be included as a separate item in the accounts. Many societies, however, still include this statement as part of the directors' report. In these circumstances, it will be necessary for the auditor's report to refer specifically to that statement.

Set out below is a form of unqualified auditor's report:

## AUDITOR'S REPORT TO THE MEMBERS OF . . . BUILDING SOCIETY

I/We have audited the financial statements on pages . . . to . . . (and the statement of source and application of funds in the directors' report) in accordance with approved Auditing Standards.

In my/our opinion the financial statements together with the statement of source and application of funds, which have been prepared under the historical cost convention (as modified by the revaluation of land and buildings), give a true and fair view of the state of the society's affairs at . . . and of its income and expenditure and source and application of funds for the year then ended, and are drawn up in accordance with the Building Societies Act 1962 and the regulations made thereunder.

### Annual Return

The matters on which the auditor must report are set out in Section 91. The auditor is required to report on, *inter alia*, any advances to directors or officers of the Society or to companies in which they are interested. The auditor will normally have to rely on information given to the Society by the directors and officers as required by Section 89. In these circumstances, the auditor should make this clear in his report.

Set out below is a form of unqualified auditor's report on the annual return subject to the reservation referred to in the previous paragraph:

AUDITOR'S REPORT ON THE ANNUAL RETURN OF THE . . . BUILDING SOCIETY FOR THE YEAR ENDED . . .

I/We have examined the foregoing annual return of the year ended . . . with the exception of the information contained in Part . . . with which I am/we are not required to deal and which accordingly my/our report does not cover. In my/our opinion the annual return (as far as I am/we are required to report on it), which has been prepared under the historical cost convention (as modified by the revaluation of land and buildings), is drawn up in accordance with the Building Societies Act 1962 and regulations made thereunder, is in agreement with the books of account and records of the society and gives a true and fair view of the matters to which it is addressed. In relation to Section B of Part 8, I/we have no information other than that disclosed by the directors and officers in accordance with Section 89(2) of the Act.

# 9  Accounting for Finance Leases

*Most examination syllabuses require students of both auditing and accounting to be aware of areas of controversy surrounding accounting treatment, whether or not an accounting standard has already been issued. Accounting for finance leases is just such an area and, at the time of writing, an exposure draft has been issued (ED29). A full Standard is scheduled for publication later in 1983.*

The latest foray by the Accounting Standards Committee (ASC) against those of who would use financial statements to dissemble reality has now been published in the form of Exposure Draft 29, entitled *Accounting for Leases and Hire Purchase Contracts*. ED29 specifies that all finance leases should be capitalised. The draft on leasing thus appears to represent yet another triumph of 'substance over form' — that is, assuming it eventually reaches full status without too many drastic changes.

## Background to UK Finance Leasing

UK legislation grants heavy tax allowances to companies investing in capital equipment, and currently the full cost is permitted as a charge against trading profits in the year of purchase. But many companies do not require these allowances, finding that their stock relief claims eliminate most of their tax charges anyway, and to such companies the 100% first year tax allowances do not therefore have a great deal of relevance.

This is one of the reasons why 'finance leasing' has become such a popular activity in recent years. The lessee company acquires the capital equipment it needs (without any major cash outlay being necessary) by leasing it from a finance house, often a subsidiary of one of the major clearing banks, and all so-called 'rental' payments become tax deductible in full. This has the effect of spreading the tax benefit over a number of accounting periods, rather than receiving all in the first year. Tax equalisation problems are thereby eased, and lessee companies are largely relieved of the trauma of having to lash out on capital goods shortly before the year end, purely to offset any unexpected taxable profit that is about to be revealed!

Another significant advantage, of course, is that the lessee company does not have to record the acquisition of the asset in its balance sheet, even though its trading results reflect the use of that asset. Nor does anything appear on the liabilities side of the balance sheet, thus contriving a favourable picture so far as both the level of borrowings and the financial gearing are concerned. For many companies, especially those already fairly heavily funded externally, this therefore represents one of the most attractive features of all.

## Advantages to the Lessor

Lessor companies, for their part, are in effect providing the finance and retaining the legal ownership, at least until the full cost of the asset and the finance and handling charges have been covered by rental payments, after which ownership may be transferred for a purely nominal sum — although in practice it is more likely that at this point the annual rentals will themselves fall to a notional figure; a clear case of possession being of more practical importance than legal title. The prime advantages for the provider of lease finance are, of course,

(a) the profitable nature of this form of financing in its own right, rental payments usually being geared to the general level of interest rates; and

(b) the entitlement to the full capital allowances to set off against taxable profits anywhere in the group.

While such an arrangement clearly suits all the parties involved (not least the manufacturers of capital goods — and hence the economy!), there is a clear conflict between the commercial substance of this type of transaction and its outward legal form; and this conflict is inevitably reflected in the question of accounting treatment. A relatively small proportion of companies (United Biscuits, to the their credit, being one) reveal this form of capital finance on the face of their balance sheets, the majority following the strict legal position, relegating the information concerned to an attenuated note, usually lost amid the welter of extraneous published data. The ASC has felt for some time that financial and taxation-based decisions should not, of themselves, determine the form of disclosure adopted in pursuing the increasingly elusive 'true and fair' view, especially when this results in utterly inconsistent methods being followed for transactions of an essentially similar nature. Under hire purchase transactions, for example, the asset is always capitalised, even though its title is not strictly transferred until it its final payment is made. On the question of accounting for the acquisition of assets, the key factor is the *intent* in the minds of the parties: if the intention is, say, to hire earth-moving equipment for the three month duration of a building programme, there is no doubt that the hire cost should be charged against profits and the balance sheet remain unaffected. The intention is clearly to return the equipment to it its owner (an equipment-hire company, not a bank!) as soon as its purpose has been served. But finance-leasing is entirely different: the intention of the lessee is to acquire the use of the equipment for the whole of its effective useful life; and the bank (the lessor), for its part, will never so much as see the equipment — still less take possession of it (except, of course, in the event of default through non-payment of 'rent').

**The Principal Obstacles to ED29**

In the evidence built up by the ASC prior to issuing ED29, four main obstacles to the capitalisation of finance leases were cited, principally by representatives of the leasing industry itself:

(a) The Revenue authorities, renowned for following the accounting treatment when it suits them to do so, might dismantle the entire tax superstructure which now exists, thereby removing the *raison d'etre* of this form of finance. In particular, the lessee (rather than the lessor) would receive the tax allowances, irrespective of whether there are sufficient profits to use them.

(b) The calculations required to capitalise leased assets are too complicated for small companies (ED29 is to apply to *all* companies, unlike its USA counterpart, FAS13, which applies to only large companies).

(c) The capitalisation of leases may put some companies in breach of their borrowing powers, which may be exceeded if the capitalised present value of future rentals is shown on the balance sheet as a liability.

(d) The need to bring such leases onto the face of the balance sheet might discourage many companies from investing in capital equipment altogether, with a detrimental effect on industry and on the economy.

While the ASC has boldly declared that it has received no convincing evidence that any of these dangers is likely to materialise, it is obvious that all will not be plain sailing. They have, however, received welcome support from investment analysts and stock brokers. Phillips & Drew, for example, have said that some companies are excessively involved as finance lessees, and that in general a lower level of leasing might be a healthy development. 'Are you sure', asked partner

Martin Gibbs, FCA, 'that it isn't a good idea to limit the number of over-geared companies to prevent the kind of situation which led to the collapse of Court Line?'.

This is a reference to the major UK travel company which failed in 1974, having significant liabilities financed by leasing which did not appear anywhere in its published financial statements.

# 10  The 'Going Concern' Checklist

*Most firms have now taken the precaution of issuing all senior audit personnel with checklists designed to test the assumption that a particular client organisation is in fact a going concern — and there is no doubt that such a checklist has become a necessity in this time of economic difficulty. The brief note which follows incorporates all the 'problem' symptoms which might be usefully examined for this particular purpose.*

Under SSAP 2, accounts are assumed to be prepared on a going concern basis unless otherwise stated. In the context of one of the worst recessions in recent history, auditors should not assume the going concern basis is appropriate for all clients — they should *confirm* that it is!

The diagnosis should begin by considering whether the client displays any of the following 'danger signals':

(a) major loan repayments are falling due in the near future;
(b) high or increasing debt to equity ratios exist (high gearing);
(c) companies are heavily or increasingly dependent upon short-term finance;
(d) there is inability to take advantage of discounts, necessity to pay on cash terms, or where the time taken to pay creditors is increasing;
(e) substantial losses are occurring, or the rate of profitability is declining;
(f) purchases are being deferred, thereby reducing stocks to dangerously low levels;
(g) necessary capital expenditure is being switched to leasing agreements;
(h) the company is in an exposed position in relation to future commitments, such as long-term assets financed by short- or medium-term borrowings;
(i) the company has a net deficiency of assets, or its ratio of current assets to current liabilities is declining;
(j) the company is near to its present borrowing limits, with no sign of a reduction in its requirements;
(k) collection from debtors is slowing down;
(l) rapid development of business creates a dangerous over-trading situation in which short-term cash requirements may not be forthcoming or available through normal channels;
(m) there is substantial investment in new products, ventures or research which are not yet successful;
(n) there is dependence on a limited number of products, customers or suppliers;
(o) there is evidence of reductions or cancellations of capital projects;
(p) there is heavy dependence on an overseas holding company (for finance or trade).

If the presence of *any* of the above factors is evident (and the list is by no means exhaustive), further steps must be taken to confirm that the client is a going concern — and not on the way out. At the very least the auditor must:

(a) compare the client's cash flow forecast with the overdraft or other loan facilities available for up to 12 months from the accounting date;
(b) if applicable, obtain written confirmation from the holding company that it intends its subsidiary to continue in business and will not withdraw finance facilities;
(c) enquire into or obtain written evidence of any steps the client is taking to correct any decline in its fortunes.

If the auditor cannot satisfy himself that the client will remain in business in the foreseeable future, then he must reconsider the validity of the going concern basis, and the possible need to qualify his audit report in appropriate terms.

## Small Companies

Particular care should be taken in reviewing small or proprietor-controlled companies, especially where there are substantial 'loans' from directors.

Such loans are often regarded as forming part of the longer-term capital of the company. For the purposes of the going concern assessment, they should be so treated only if they are legally subordinated to all other creditors. There should be adequate disclosure of the position.

Where directors' loans rank *pari passu* with other unsecured creditors, they should be treated as ordinary current liabilities. This will help to emphasise any deficiency of assets as regards unsecured creditors unless other financial support has been arranged, and will indicate that the going concern basis of valuation of assets may not be applicable.

# 11 Audits of Small Companies

*Prior to the adoption (in the form of the Companies Act 1981) of the EEC Fourth Directive, the question of the necessity for small companies (now defined in Section 8 of the Act) to be subject to audit requirements was hotly debated. Although there is now some relaxation of small company filing regulations, the audit requirement persists. In reality, of course, what passes as an audit for many such companies generally comprises the preparation of the accounts by the auditor, clearly acting in an accounting capacity. The question which always arises is whether this arrangement is satisfactory, and whether a formal audit, in such cases, can be realistically attempted at all. One is also left with the question of how far it is possible for a set of accounts to be independently audited by the person who has prepared them. The notes which follow summarise this continuing debate, a favourite theme for professional examiners.*

## Background to the Debate

The application of auditing standards to the audit of small companies managed and owned by substantially the same people is a subject the Auditing Practices Committee has under continuous consideration. A fundamental question in this context is whether the value derived from the audit of such a company is commensurate with the cost of carrying it out.

From the point of view of the *proprietor* there is clearly an advantage in having accounts properly prepared but the additional advantage of having them audited is marginal. The same applies to the other *shareholders* who are usually small in number and closely connected with the proprietor.

The *creditor* derives some benefit but, since accounts are often filed many months after a company's year end, those providing credit more often resort to trade sources for more up-to-date information on the company's creditworthiness. *Employees*, also by reason of their small number and the simple management structure, are frequently in a position to guess reasonably at the trading position of the business.

These are some of the arguments which lead to a view that there is less need for the audit of small *proprietary* companies than for others.

When it comes to *auditing standards* there are other factors leading to the same conclusions. The proprietor will usually look to his auditor for help in all financial matters: tax, preparation of accounts, assistance in negotiating additional finance, etc. The auditor, in examining these areas, will thus be auditing his own work; can he therefore be truly independent? If the accountant and the auditor should not be the same person the cost of the audit increases. A further problem is whether sufficient corroborative evidence exists in a small company for the auditor to form an opinion as to whether or not all the transactions have been recorded.

The problem could be resolved by allowing *different audit standards* to be applied to different types of company. To differentiate between the two, the auditor's report would have to make it clear which standards had been applied and this could quickly lead to misunderstanding and the application of inappropriate standards. The law presently requires auditors of *all* companies to form an opinion as to whether the accounts give a true and fair view without regard to the relative sizes of clients. Dual standards are not only far from an ideal solution, but also arguably illegal.

There is therefore a strong case for *changing the law*, perhaps when the overdue Companies Acts consolidation takes place, to allow shareholders of smaller companies to *choose* whether they wish to have their companies' accounts audited (which, incidentally, would not be out of step with practice and developments in other countries). If they so choose there would still need to be a requirement for some form of report (in less stringent terms than at present) to be given by a qualified accountant so that the accounts may have the necessary level of authority to creditors, minority shareholders, the Inland Revenue and other third parties. It should not be imagined, however, that such a change would be applicable to all private companies; many private companies are of a substantial size and have several outside interests in the form of trade creditors, providers of long-term finance, and minority shareholders. These interests would clearly continue to require the assurance provided by an independent audit. But a change may be applied to 'proprietary' companies, which for this purpose may be regarded as those in which all the directors are shareholders, and all the shareholders are directors. Such a change would bring the UK into line with most other developed nations in requiring statutory audits for certain companies only, leaving the matter discretionary for smaller companies, usually at the option of their shareholders.

## The Argument 'For' and 'Against'

The principal arguments in favour of *abolishing* audit requirements for small companies may be summarised as follows.

(a) Proprietors of such companies tend to require financial services (book-keeping, tax advice, etc.) from professional accountants, and regard the audit aspect of the work as part of the price of incorporation, but of no immediate value.

(b) Since the shareholders and directors are the same people, there is something ludicrous about the spectacle of 'directors' supplying information to the auditor so that the latter is then in a position to report back to them with their 'shareholder hats' on.

(c) There is no legal requirement for outside interests to be served by the auditor and, in any case, such outsiders make no contribution to the audit fee.

(d) Many outside interests such as banks are well protected by personal guarantees from directors and charges against company assets. They are therefore not dependent on the audit for protection.

(e) Creditors are able to make little use of the audit since the accounts and audit report are filed many months after credit is given and such accounts, even if fully understood, would therefore provide little indication of the risks involved.

The arguments in favour of *retaining* the audit, on the other hand, may be summarised as follows.

(a) Outside interests do in fact pay a price for dealing with limited liability companies in that the shareholders/directors may select their moment for putting the company into liquidation at little or no cost to themselves, and to the exclusive detriment of unprotected trade creditors. The possibility of such an action represents the supreme privilege of incorporation, and the audit therefore represents a vital safeguard against its abuse.

(b) Although the law fails to acknowledge any duty of care to outsiders on the part of the auditor, such a duty may reasonably be inferred from the requirement under the Companies Act 1967 that all companies previously exempt from so doing are required to publish their audited accounts, together with their annual return, by filing them at Companies House. There is thus a clear inference that outsiders may rely upon such filed accounts for any reasonable purpose, and recent case law on auditors' liability to third parties seems to confirm this (see chapter 4).

(c) Although the arguments concerning late filing are appreciated, it is quite incorrect to equate the value of the audit as a whole with the value of the audit report — often regarded as a formality and of academic interest. It is the audit *presence* which imposes a major discipline on corporate conduct, and which constitutes one of the most significant safeguards of the interests of all those who do business with incorporated entities. It is therefore likely that delinquency and mismanagement would, to an unquantifiable degree, result from a complete removal of the audit discipline.

## The Audit as a Safeguard

The mere audit presence acts as a moral check upon the client's staff and on the procedures they follow. The knowledge that the records are subsequently to be subjected to an independent check, the timing and extent of which remain largely unknown to staff and officers alike, acts as a far more powerful spur to the honest, industrious and accurate performance of managerial and clerical tasks than we within the profession perhaps realise.

Directors of client companies, moreover, are constrained in some measure by the stipulations of company law on capital preservation, the maintenance and retention of up-to-date records, filing of accounts and annual returns, conduct of meetings and recording of proceedings in formal minutes, and a host of other equally important matters, which collectively impose a discipline on the conduct of business affairs. The auditor, indirectly perhaps, ensures wherever possible that these disciplines are observed.

It is fashionable to be cynical these days, and point to the innumerable instances where the incompetent or delinquent behaviour of corporate officers has passed unhampered by auditors and all the other regulatory measures provided by law and by custom; thereby suggesting that their ineffectiveness should signal their own demise. Yet of one thing we may be certain: without an audit presence such abuses would be greater, and failures vastly more common. The rule, even, rather than the exception. And the prime sufferers when a company collapses, let us remind ourselves, are invariably the unsecured trade creditors.

For all those who would trade with incorporated entities, the audit requirement should therefore continue to afford a measure of assurance that they are not embarking on a one-way ride to financial loss. And such assurance should be provided irrespective of who reads or heeds a mechanically drafted audit report.

## Review or Audit?

Although there has been much discussion concerning the substitution of a 'review' for a full-scale audit, no clear definition has been given of what such a review would entail. If the Canadian system is followed, a review would comprise a rigorous investigation of the company's published accounts with special reference to comparisons with earlier periods and with other businesses in the same trade, including an analysis of ratios, trends and forecasts. A review would, however, normally exclude many basic verification procedures covering inspection of physical stocks, plant and machinery and other tangible assets; inspection of basic documentary evidence, so far as this may reasonably be made available, would nevertheless normally be examined. Under the terms of the Canadian approach, as formulated by the Canadian Institute of Chartered Accountants, the aim of the review is to establish no more than the *plausibility* (or otherwise) of the financial statements of the enterprise. The question of whether a comprehensive review of the accounts and records should be substituted for a full-scale audit for proprietary companies in the UK will no doubt continue to be debated in the years to come, but the Companies Act 1981 has, temporarily at least, settled the immediate issue.

## An Independent View

Following an invitation by the APC to express views on this subject, one international firm responded substantially as follows:

## Should Mandatory Audits Continue for Small Companies?

1. It is our view that because the directors of small companies exercise 'proprietorial' control, usually little value is gained by members from an independent audit opinion. The original aim of the audit function was to give the members of a company comfort regarding the management's stewardship of their company during the period under review. When, as is generally so in small companies, the proprietors also manage the company we doubt whether there is any value in an independent audit opinion that is addressed to members.

2. It is often impossible for auditors to obtain adequate assurance on internal control or documentary evidence to verify transactions, particularly those that involve cash. Consequently, following the introduction of auditing standards, it is likely that many auditor's reports on small companies will need to be qualified. We believe that the plethora of qualified accounts that would then result would be unhelpful, and so we consider that the financial statements of small companies should not be subject to a statutory requirement for audit. This view is held by a majority of partners in our firm.

3. We believe that, in practice, many small companies would choose to continue to have their financial statements audited. Many boards of directors would desire to have an independent opinion, and debenture holders, mortgagees and bankers would also require the assurance of an audit opinion (even though on occasions that opinion might be qualified).

4. We believe, also, that an audit should be conducted if the holders of more than a specified percentage of the company's share capital request it. If that percentage were set at 10% the rights of the minority shareholders would be afforded reasonable protection.

5. We consider that, at the date of the annual general meeting at which the financial statements of the previous period are considered, the members of the company should decide whether or not the financial statements for the current period are to be audited. Shareholders should, however, have the right to convene an extraordinary meeting at a later date for the purpose of requesting an audit on the financial statements of a current period.

6. We are of course aware that where the members of a company request an audit, and where the financial statements of the previous financial period have not been audited, the auditor may not be able to express an unqualified opinion on the profit and loss account for the current period. This is because he may not be able to obtain audit satisfaction on the opening balances for the period on which he is reporting.

## Should Small Company Financial Statements be Reviewed?

7. If the mandatory audit requirement were removed, we do not consider that review procedures offer a practicable alternative. To obtain the required level of assurance, the reviewer's approach would not be materially different to the auditor's approach. He would be required to apply standards which tested the truth and fairness of the accounts and, in so doing he would perform substantially the same tests as he would if he was performing a statutory audit. We consider that a review would not be practicable because:

(a) It would be difficult to define the level of assurance that would result from such a review.
(b) By definition, a review must contain qualifications, and these reduce its value.
(c) It would be difficult to avoid misleading the public as to the status of review. Inevitably, it would in time take on the status of a statutory audit.

This view is almost unanimous within our firm.

## Definition of a 'Small Company'

8. It has been suggested that the bottom tier of companies as defined by the Companies Act 1981 should be the criteria that should be used for defining the small company for audit purposes. We agree with this suggestion in principle.

## General

The following additional points were made by many of our partners:

(a) If the requirement for a mandatory audit were removed, directors should be required to make a positive statement that, in their opinion, the accounts give a true and fair view.

(b) It should be made easier for companies to revert to unlimited status without causing them difficulties as regards administration and taxation.

# 12   Current Cost Accounting and the Auditor

*In their publication* True and Fair *the Auditing Practices Committee of the CCAB published a short article on which the following notes are based, indicating the effect of Current Cost Accounting on the conduct of the audit. Although SSAP 16 is still operative at the time of writing (being half-way through its three year experimental period) a good deal of opposition to its mandatory enforcement is being voiced. A recent (July 1982) vote on the subject showed that only 50% of Institute members favour its continuation. It is no secret that even within the Auditing Practices Committee there is a decided lack of unanimity on the extent to which CCA can in fact be 'audited'. In the meanwhile, it is worth noting the recommendations of the APC referred to later in this chapter, which, in general terms, remain valid for supplementary statements prepared under SSAP 16.*

The publicity attending the publication of the report of the Sandilands Committee, the work of the Inflation Accounting Steering Group and the subsequent publication of SSAP 16, *Current Cost Accounting*, have created in some quarters the fear that the introduction of current cost accounting will change overnight all the procedures familiar to an auditor in the course of his work. This is not true. The bulk of the work carried out by an auditor is unaffected by the introduction of current cost accounting. Clients' staff will still be occupied in buying goods, paying wages and invoicing sales and all of these will require auditing as in the past.

Similarly, in auditing the balance sheet, the auditor will still be examining assets from the point of view of the authority for their purchase, evidence of their existence and of their ownership; the aspect of assets which will change on the introduction of current cost accounting will be the examination of the value at which they are stated.

The essence of the CCA convention is extremely simple, namely to adjust income, in arriving at the CCA profit for the year, for:

(a) the value to the business, at the date of the consumption rather than at the date of purchase, of stocks consumed;

(b) the impact of price changes on monetary working capital;

(c) depreciation equal to that proportion of the fixed assets' value to the business (as opposed to historical cost) which is being consumed during the year; and

(d) the extent to which (a), (b) and (c) above are affected by the relationship of shareholders' equity to total funding.

Since balance sheets have in recent years often reflected the revaluation of certain assets, the significance of CCA for users of published accounts and thus for the auditor will be reflected more in the profit and loss account than in the balance sheet.

Some of the principal areas in which they will need to take account of changes in accounting principles are:

*Fixed Assets.* With the introduction of a new basis for the valuation of fixed assets in the balance sheet the auditor needs a deeper knowledge of the basic decision-making process of management as to the use, suitability and expected life span of major items of plant and machinery. Such study will be essential if the auditor is going to be able to assess adequately whether or not the basis of valuation, as proposed by management, is supported by acceptable opinions and evidence and is in accordance with the principles laid down in the Standard.

*Deferred taxation.* In determining the amount to be provided for the deferred tax liability the standard introduces the consideration, as yet undefined, of 'reasonable probability' and 'foreseeable future', in assessing the amount to be provided for the deferred tax liability.

*Transfer to reserves.* The directors will determine, from the CCA supplementary statement, the extent to which the company's current cost reserves require to be adjusted each year, and will explain the basis of their calculations and their reasons either in the directors' report or in the notes to the accounts.

*Distributable profits.* Much of the law on distributable profits originates from cases in the early part of this century and is neither codified nor precise. Updated legislation in this area has been urgently required, and the advent of CCA makes it even more important. Major changes on this front have already been introduced in Sections 39 to 43 of the Companies Act 1980, and reference should be made to the section on this development in Chapter 1.

A familiarity with CCA principles as implemented under SSAP 16 is of considerable importance to auditors, and for this purpose reference should be made to the appropriate section of Chapter 21.

## The Audit Report

The following sections are extracts from the guideline issued by the APC on the drafting of audit reports on current cost financial statements.

'This auditing guideline is intended to assist auditors when reporting on statements produced by enterprises in accordance with statement of standard accounting practice No. 16 *Current Cost Accounting* (SSAP 16). It should be read in conjunction with the explanatory foreword to Auditing Standards and guidelines (including the glossary of terms) and the auditing standards on the audit report and qualifications in audit reports.

'An enterprise will, when complying with SSAP 16, provide current cost accounting (CCA) information in one of the following forms:

(a) the presentation of historical cost accounts as the main accounts with supplementary current cost accounts which are prominently displayed,

(b) the presentation of current cost accounts as the main accounts with supplementary historical cost accounts, or

(c) the presentation of current cost accounts as the only accounts accompanied by adequate historical cost information.

'However, in the early years of CCA it is expected that many enterprises will continue to present historical cost accounts as the main accounts. In such cases the current cost accounts will be supplementary to the financial statements on which the auditor reports in accordance with any statutory obligation.

## Supplementary Current Cost Accounts

'In the case of those enterprises which have developed an appreciation for CCA as a whole and its application in their particular circumstances, they will be in a position to prepare true and fair current cost accounts. Where these are supplementary, but nevertheless complete current cost accounts, the auditor should report in true and fair terms in an additional paragraph to the report on the historical cost accounts as follows.

In our opinion the supplementary current cost accounts set out on pages . . . to . . . have been prepared in accordance with the accounting policies and methods described in notes . . . to . . . and give, under the current cost principles described in SSAP 16, a true and fair view of the state of the company's affairs at 31 December 19 . . and of its results for the year then ended.

'However, in the case of many enterprises the objective of preparing CCA accounts which give a true and fair view will not be achievable until they have developed the necessary appreciation and experience. The preparers of the current cost accounts of these enterprises will not therefore be in a position to claim that their supplementary current cost accounts do give a true and fair view.

'It follows that it will not be appropriate for the auditor to report on such supplementary current cost accounts in true and fair terms. Nevertheless, in these cases it will be helpful to the user of current cost accounts to know whether, in the opinion of the auditor, the accounting policies and procedures adopted comply with the provisions of SSAP 16. Therefore it is recommended that in these cases the auditor's report be expressed in terms which confirm "compliance" and be set out in an additional paragraph to his report on the historical cost statements.

'A form of wording which will be suitable for "compliance" reports is: "In our opinion the supplementary current cost accounts set out on pages . . . to . . . have been properly prepared, in accordance with the policies and methods described in notes . . . to . . ., to give the information required by statement of standard accounting practice No. 16'.

### Main Current Cost Accounts

'When reporting on current cost accounts which are the main or only accounts, it will not normally be necessary to make separate reference to the historical cost information presented either in the form of supplementary statements or in the form of additional notes. Nevertheless, the scope paragraph of the audit report should make clear that such information has been subjected to examination by the auditor.

### Failure to Present Current Cost Accounts

'Where an enterprise to which SSAP 16 applies does not present current cost accounts, it is not appropriate, merely, because of this omission, for the auditor to qualify his opinion on the historical cost accounts. However, he should refer to the omission using wording on the following lines for an additional paragraph to his report: "The financial statements do not contain the current cost accounts required by statement of standard accounting practice No. 16".'

### Full Current Cost Accounts — Additional Audit Work

The following is an abbreviated audit programme of additional work to be performed when the client company produces full current cost financial statements for the first time.

(a) Ensure that the accounting System from which CC data is drawn is sufficiently reliable as a basis for preparing full CC financial statements, with special reference to
  (i) recording the issue of materials at current replacement costs, as opposed to original historic costs;
  (ii) the ease with which CC of materials in stock at year end may be determined for inclusion in CC accounts.
(b) Execute audit tests on above records for the specific purpose of determining their reliability. (Since no prior data are available the level of such tests will obviously depend on findings as the auditors proceed.)
(c) If cost of sales is converted from HC to CC by means of an index, audit tests should be directed to ascertain
  (i) the general suitability and comprehensiveness of the index used, and

(ii) the accuracy with which it has been applied to records of purchases, sales, and movement of materials in store.

Although the use of such an index is convenient, it is possible that an industrial index covering prices of the particular materials involved does not yet exist. Reference to the company's technical department should be made for this purpose.

(d) Fixed assets and depreciation will be based on current replacement costs. Audit tests should ensure that such adjustments are supported by appropriate independent valuations, suppliers' price lists, etc.; and that the incidence of depreciation accords with requirements of SSAP 12, as adapted to CCA.

(e) Check basis method, and accuracy of other adjustments for monetary working capital, and the effect on these adjustments (and on those for cost of sales and depreciation already referred to) of the company's gearing ratio, as allowed by SSAP 16.

(f) Ensure that the CC Accounting Policies are sound, and reflect the CC method adopted; where appropriate, auditors should assess whether the 'economic value to the business' might, if lower than CC carried forward, be a more appropriate valuation basis.

# 13  Questionable Payments by Clients and Related Party Transactions

*A good deal of publicity has been given in recent years to cases of corporate bribery. As new situations arise auditors are obliged to adapt their audit approach, techniques and procedures, so that the unchanging objectives of the audit are maintained fully in view. The two sections which follow outline the appropriate audit attitudes and procedures in relation to*
  (a) *questionable payments by client companies; and*
  (b) *corporate transactions which may appear to be conducted on terms which are less than 'arm's length'.*


### 'Questionable' Payments by Clients

With recent increases in oil prices, certain oil producing nations have found themselves with foreign purchasing power to a degree previously unknown; in order to do business in 'oil rich' countries some companies have found it necessary or expedient to resort to the payment of bribes to individuals believed to be ideally placed for the purpose. Such payments are usually discovered during detailed testing procedures by the senior in charge of an audit or his assistants. When audit procedures bring any such payments to light, they should immediately be brought to the attention of both the manager and the partner responsible for the audit of the client organisation.

Where such payments have been made by a subsidiary company, its auditors should immediately inform the holding company auditors, who should, in turn, inform the directors of the holding company. The auditors should also ensure that the directors of the subsidiary have informed the directors of the holding company of the existence of the payments.

It should be recognised that, in many countries, such payments are part of normal business practices and, accordingly, when such payments arise, the auditors' policy should be:

  (a) to ensure that the payments were actually received by the individual specified;
  (b) that they were made wholly in connection with the furtherance of the client's business operations; and
  (c) that they have been approved by each director of the company and, where appropriate, of the holding company.

A suitable form of representation might be:

'We confirm that the payment of £x made on 15 October 1982 to Simon Palm was made wholly in connection with the company's business operations in *xxx* land.
                    *Signed* — Each director of the holding company.'

Where the conditions outlined above are satisfied, and a suitable representation has been received, disclosure in the published accounts would not normally be required, unless the sums involved are so material that their disclosure is necessary for the purpose of showing a true and fair view.

Where payments have been made by a subsidiary and the holding company is audited by *another* firm, the subsidiary auditors should ask the directors of the subsidiary to inform the directors of the holding company of the existence of the payments.

## Related Party Transactions

'Related party' transactions require special attention and scrutiny by the auditor since the terms and conditions of these transactions may be unduly favourable to one of the parties.

Depending upon the circumstances and materiality of the transactions concerned, the auditor may wish to consider the adequacy of the disclosure of these transactions in the accounts. For example, the Companies Act 1980 requires disclosure in the accounts of significant contracts in which directors have a material interest, but apart from such statutory provisions the auditor may take the view that fuller disclosure of related party transactions in the accounts is required to enable them to show a true and fair view.

The following might be included within a *definition* of related parties:

(a) organisations under common control with the client company (regarding 'control' as the power to direct management and policy through ownership, contract or otherwise);
(b) shareholders with substantial holdings of voting shares (exceeding, say, 10%);
(c) the executive directors and their immediate families;
(d) associated companies;
(e) any other party which has the ability to prevent the company from pursuing its own interests independently.

The following *types of transaction* may indicate to an auditor the existence of related parties:

(a) borrowing/lending at rates of interest substantially higher/lower than current market rates;
(b) sales/purchases of assets at prices substantially different from those currently ruling;
(c) straightforward exchanges of assets in a manner which masks the underlying value of the assets exchanged;
(d) granting of loans with no scheduled repayment terms, against little or no security.

## Identification of Related Parties

The auditor should:

(a) evaluate the company's own procedures, if any, for identifying and properly accounting for related party transactions;
(b) enquire of appropriate management personnel for the names of all known related parties, and details of any transactions with these parties during the period;
(c) review the annual return to ascertain in which *other* companies directors hold directorships;
(d) find out the names of all pension funds connected with the company, and the names of their fund managers;
(e) review the register of substantial shareholders to identify shareholders with more than, say, 10% of the voting shares;
(f) review material investment transactions during the period to determine whether the nature and extent of investments create related parties.

## Audit Procedures

All audit staff members should be supplied with the names of the related parties so that during their examinations they may become aware of transactions with the parties which give rise to special consideration.

The following additional steps should also be carried out:

(a) The minutes of meetings of the board of directors and executive or operating committees should be examined to identify any material transactions authorised or discussed.

(b) Consideration should be given to whether free accounting, management or other services are provided or received, or whether a major shareholder absorbs company expenses.

(c) Bills from solicitors or counsel who have performed regular or special services for the company should be reviewed for indications of related party transactions.

(d) Confirmations of loans receivable and payable should be examined for indications of guarantees. When such guarantees are found the relationship of the guarantors to the company should be established.

(e) Obtain an understanding of the real purpose of the transactions and the underlying substance of the transactions, rather than their legal form.

(f) Confirm transaction amounts and items, including guarantees and other significant data with the other party or parties to the transaction, where appropriate.

(g) Confirm significant information with intermediaries such as banks, guarantors, agents or solicitors to obtain a better understanding of the transactions concerned.

(h) Refer to financial publications, trade journals, credit agencies and other information sources if there is reason to believe that customers, suppliers or other organisations with which material amounts of business have been transacted may lack substance.

(i) Obtain, in respect of material uncollected balances, guarantees and other obligations, information as to the financial standing of the other party or parties. Such information may be obtained from audited accounts, management accounts, financial publications and credit agencies.

The Companies Act 1980 requires the disclosure of significant contracts in which directors have a material interest. It should be remembered that a 'director' is deemed to include any person in accordance with whose directions or instructions the employees of the company are accustomed to act. In some circumstances it may therefore be necessary to disclose material related party transactions in the accounts, so as to show a true and fair view.

**Typical Examination Questions**

Most Advanced Auditing examination papers now include one or more questions of a 'mini-case study' type, clearly involving related parties, and students are expected to annotate the further enquiries which an auditor should make in the circumstances, as well as the audit evidence he would seek. It should be remembered that related party transactions are not illegal — the questions which arise relate purely to disclosure in the accounts. Many related party situations result in one or more companies within a group incurring expenditure at a level which exceeds what would be incurred if they were dealing with outsiders on an arm's length basis. In such situations it is of paramount importance for the auditor to ensure (a) that all directors of the companies adversely affected are fully aware of the situation and that the amounts have been quantified so far as possible; and (b) that the position of minority interests has been considered. Where an auditor is responsible for the accounts of a subsidiary thus adversely affected, he has a primary duty to ensure that minority interests in that subsidiary are made aware of the position in the notes to the accounts or, if necessary, in the auditor's report.

Accounts which do no more than reflect the trading results in terms of accurate monetary amounts cannot be said to give a *fair* as well as a *true* view, since they give no indication of profitability/net asset levels attainable in circumstances in which all transactions with outsiders are conducted at arm's length.

# 14   Audit Committees as an Aid to Independence

*Following the recent mandatory stipulation in the USA that quoted companies, as a condition of listing, will be required to appoint independent Audit Committees, this matter is being given careful consideration in the UK.*

## Background

If the uncomfortable episodes in which auditors have recently been involved serve no purpose other than to force us to look really thoroughly at the whole question of independence, they will have been worthwhile.

A disinterested study of this matter must necessarily begin with the question of exactly what we mean by 'independent', and its very simplicity makes it exceedingly difficult to answer. One thing, however, is clear: the essential attribute of what we mean when we use this word, is independence of *mind*.

Some may ask whether the issue is worth all the fuss, whether independence is really so essential. To that there is a simple answer: the concept of the auditor and the concept of independence are the twin sides of the same coin. The auditor who has lost his independence has lost his *raison d'être*;he has become dependent, and a 'dependent auditor' is a contradiction in terms.

Those situations which have the effect of undermining the auditor's independence are many and various. They do, however, all have one distinguishing feature in common: they are all situations in which there is an implicit temptation on the part of the auditor to avoid incurring the displeasure of those able to sack him.

One current proposal which merits very serious (and urgent) attention advocates the establishment, initially for all listed companies, of an independent 'audit committee', chiefly comprising *non-executive* officers of the company, appointed to view the company's position in a detached and dispassionate light, and to liaise effectively between its main board and its external auditors. Since the final form and function of such a committee is still a matter for debate, it would be quite misleading to attempt too close a definition; the following activities have, however, been associated with it:

(a) to review formally and regularly the financial results shown by both management accounts and those presented to shareholders;
(b) to make recommendations for the improvement of management control;
(c) to assist external auditors in obtaining all the information they require and in resolving any difficulties experienced by them in pursuing their independent examination;
(d) to deal with any material reservations of the auditors regarding the company's management, its records and its final accounts, including the manner in which significant items are presented therein;
(e) to facilitate a satisfactory working relationship between the management and auditors, and between the internal and external audit functions;
(f) to ensure that there are adequate procedures for reviewing 'rights' circulars, interim statements, forecasts, and other financial information prior to distribution to shareholders.

## The USA Comparison

Often what we in the UK consider to be a novel development is in fact something which our North

American colleagues have debated long and hard for years, even decades; and the question of audit committees is no exception. Both the Securities and Exchange Commission (SEC) and the New York Stock Exchange (NYSE) first recommended the institution of audit committees in 1940. This recommendation was followed by several companies, but only gained real momentum in 1967, when the American Institute of Certified Public Accountants acted positively by recommending that 'publicly owned corporations appoint committees composed of outside directors to nominate the independent auditors . . . and to discuss the auditors' work with them'.

In 1972 and 1973, in the wake of the Equity Funding fraud scandal, both the SEC and NYSE put further pressure on company boards to appoint audit committees, culminating in the September 1976 bulletin of the NYSE sent to the chief executives of all listed companies which, after pointing out that over 80% of public companies already have audit committees, made clear its intention to require the presence of such a committee as a condition of listing after 31 December 1977.

When contrasting these North American developments with our domestic situation, two aspects are striking: (a) whereas in the USA and Canada the initiative has been taken by the professional bodies and regulatory agencies, culminating in compliance by companies, in the UK only the voice of Sir Brandon Rhys Williams MP has, despite endless frustration, tirelessly pleaded the case for audit committees, against the usual background of lethargy and complacency on the part of those government departments and professional bodies now being forced to recognise the wisdom of his perennial private members Bills; and (b) although there is currently no lack of controversy concerning the role and standard of auditing in the USA, little of it surrounds the independence issue.

The need for audit committees, or their UK counterpart, is clear and it is often suggested that, in addition to the matters already listed, they should:

(a) be responsible for the appointment of auditors, as well as fixing their remuneration;
(b) be available for consultation with the auditors at all times, if necessary without the presence of management;
(c) regularly discuss and review the procedures employed by the auditors; and
(d) be concerned with all matters relating to the disclosure by the accounts of a true and fair view for the benefits of all users.

**Arguments against Audit Committees**

Against the persuasive arguments set out above, the following should also be borne in mind:

(a) There is in the UK very little definition given to the optimum constitution and function of an audit committee, and those public companies who have voluntarily appointed such committees have done so on a variety of bases. Furthermore, there is little collective experience upon which to base an evaluation of their usefulness and effectiveness, either as an aid to the independence of external auditors or as a means of controlling the excesses of senior corporate executives. It may therefore be validly argued that at least ten more years of experience on an experimental basis are needed before the concept of audit committees should be given statutory support.
(b) The attempts by Sir Brandon Rhys Williams to introduce audit committees have been based on a concept somewhat different from that normally adopted. His chief aim appears to be to appoint 'watchdog' shareholder committees, whose purpose would be to maintain a watching brief over the activities of the main board, and would probably incorporate an audit of corporate objectives and achievements. The more usual concept of audit committees is clearly rather different, and it may be that his efforts (including the use of the name 'audit committees') may turn out to have been counter-productive in progressing the adoption of this idea.

(c) The wider experience of audit committees on the North American Continent is itself inconclusive, in so far as the audit committee is supposed to monitor and control the conduct of dominating company directors; certainly, external auditors appear to be no better protected by the presence of such committees against threats of removal every time they appear to make a stand on questions of disclosure and accounting treatment. Doubts therefore remain concerning the independence of the audit committee itself, and whether it can ever, on a part-time, non-executive basis, exercise the degree of influence over senior full-time directors for which its presence is created in the first place.

(d) Justifiable fears also exist that a powerful audit committee may serve to hamper executive flair which, by its very nature, will always appear to contravene accepted norms. As in any other area of human activity, innovation and experimentation are vital to successful commercial enterprise, in the face of which a non-executive audit committee (whose members are concerned to avoid risks and keep low profiles) may be more akin to a millstone than a spur.

(e) Audit committees, if made mandatory for public companies, might provide an entirely false sense of security for shareholders and external auditors alike. In many cases, the result would be the creation of either an expensive, yet ineffectual, rubber-stamping exercise or an unwarranted brake on the enterprising flair of the more gifted members of the board.

# 15   Reservation of Title Clauses

*There has been considerable debate over the extent to which the controversial 1976 Romalpa case should be heeded by commercial enterprises, their professional advisers and their auditors. The outcome of this, and other more recent cases, affects the legal position of parties to a contract involving sale of goods in instances where the terms of the contract are intended to ensure that the seller retains the title to the goods until payment in full has been received. It provides the arena for one of the classic contests between 'legal form' and 'commercial substance', and the notes which follow deal with the respective positions of the supplying and purchasing companies, disclosure requirements, and audit implications.*

The Romalpa case (*Aluminium Industrie Vaassen BV v. Romalpa Aluminium Limited*) decided in the Court of Appeal on 16 January 1976 has many implications for auditors whose clients purchase goods or sell them subject to reservation of title. While the terms of sale in such transactions may vary from case to case, the general effect is that the seller retains title over the goods sold, until paid for, and may even have rights over other goods produced from them, and over the ultimate sale proceeds.

Banks and others who lend money secured by a floating charge are vitally concerned with the strength of the borrower's balance sheet, and the inclusion in stock of an unrecognised value of goods purchased under Romalpa-type contracts could seriously undermine their security. Where both the company and auditors fail to detect and indicate the amount included as part of creditors which is protected by such clauses, they could be laying themselves open to serious trouble if the company fails and its suppliers exercise their rights.

Clearly, therefore, the auditor has a responsibility to enquire whether the client purchases goods from suppliers on terms which include reservation of title by the suppliers and, if the answer is in the affirmative, to review the client's procedures for accounting for such transactions.

The Institute, in V 24, has issued a guidance statement which points out the need to decide at what stage such goods should treated as sold by the supplier, and as purchased by the purchasing company. *In reaching this decision, it is considered that the commercial substance of the transaction should take precedence over its legal form.* If the circumstances indicate that the reservation of title is regarded by the client company as having no practical relevance (except in the event of the insolvency of the purchasing company) then it is recommended that, to give a true and fair view, goods should be treated as *purchases in the accounts of the purchasing company, and as sales in the accounts of the supplier* (i.e. a *commercial* basis).

*Note*: If the financial position of the purchasing company throws doubt on the going concern concept, the accounting treatment of goods supplied on such terms will need particular consideration. In the rare circumstances that the accounts have been drawn up on some basis other than the going concern basis, it would be necessary to have regard to the strict legal position in relation to the transaction.

**Disclosure**

There are two matters that may require to be disclosed in the accounts:

(a) *Accounting Policy*. If the accounts are materially affected by the accounting treatment adopted in relation to sales or purchases subject to reservation of title, the policy adopted should be disclosed.

(b) *Secured Liability*. Where, as would normally be the case, the commercial basis has been adopted, the accounts of the purchasing company should disclose that liabilities, subject to the reservation of title, are secured. The secured liability should be quantified in the accounts.

## Taxation Implications

The Inland Revenue has stated that, so long as both parties adopt the commercial basis recommended in the English Institute's statement, they will accept this basis for taxation purposes. If, however, either party draws up its tax computation or accounts on the legal basis, the Revenue reserve the right to insist on the legal basis being adopted by both parties.

## Audit Implications

Auditors of the *purchasing company* should adopt the following procedures:

(a) Ascertain from the directors, and from those responsible for purchasing, what steps they have taken to identify suppliers selling on terms subject to reservation of title.

(b) Review the steps taken to quantify the secured liability to suppliers at the balance sheet date, including goods not yet invoiced at that date.

(c) Examine the conditions of sale laid down by suppliers selected for testing. Where these tests identify creditors who have supplied goods subject to reservation of title, check that the disclosed year end secured liability to these creditors is correctly stated.

(d) Where there are material secured liabilities to suppliers:
  (i) ensure that these liabilities are stated as being secured in the accounts;
  (ii) ensure that the relevant accounting policy has been disclosed in the accounts.

(e) Obtain formal written representation, in the Letter of Representation, from the directors either that there are no material liabilities of this nature to be disclosed, or that the amount is fully disclosed in the accounts.

To auditors of the *supplying* company, reservation of title will be relevant only in considering the valuation of the debt. Where a provision for bad or doubtful debts is contemplated, the ability to recover the goods may have some bearing on the value of the debt.

## Legal Background

There is in fact nothing new about retention of title. The Sale of Goods Act 1893 specifically provides for it and in some trade sectors these clauses have been common. In Europe sellers take active steps to impose terms of this kind, and with an increase in inter-EEC trade, UK traders must understand the consequence of agreeing to a contract term of this kind.

Put at its simplest, the seller says 'I will supply you with these goods for you to sell but I will retain legal ownership of them until you have paid me in full for *everything* supplied'. Thus the purchaser has no legal ownership at any time even if the goods are received and resold, until he pays for them. The ultimate buyer *does* get good title, however, unless he is aware of the retention of title clause. For a retailer not to own the goods means that he cannot use them as security for an overdraft or floating charges; nor can his creditors seize the goods. So credit may be difficult to obtain, and a receiver's job becomes a nightmare.

However, it is essential that the clause is drafted in crystal clear terms, particularly where the goods being sold are not finished goods to be resold as they stand, but raw materials to be incorporated in the manufacture of a product. In each of the important recent cases the seller sought to protect itself in case the buyer defaulted on the payment of goods sold, and the goods were to be added by the purchaser to other goods in a process of manufacture, thus losing their original identity.

In the *Romalpa* case, the Dutch seller had retained legal title to aluminium foil by express reservation until it was paid all money due to it from the buyer. The seller was entitled to recover all unused or unsold foil if the buyer defaulted and, as the clause had imposed on the buyer a duty to account to the seller for the proceeds of sale of all unmixed foil, it was held that the buyer was fully accountable to the seller who had priority over all other creditors. Although the *Romalpa* clause was worded tortuously (and was not improved by translation) it was extremely effective because the buyer was treated as the agent for the seller until such time as he had paid for all aluminium foil with which he had been supplied.

In *Borden (UK) Ltd. v. Scottish Timber Products Ltd.* another retention of title clause was scrutinised on an appeal against a decision upholding its validity. Borden sold resin to the defendants who used it with other products to make chipboard. The clause said that the property in the resin being sold would pass only when the goods comprised in the contract had been paid for in full. The lower court implied a licence on the part of the buyer to use the resin to make chipboard and held that the seller had no title to the chipboard in which the resin had been incorporated. What the seller did have, said the judge, was an equitable right to trace the proceeds of sale of the resin and chipboard mixture. The Appeal Court gave short shrift to this argument. Once used, the resin was completely changed in character and it was quite impossible to recover it. The resin no longer existed and the Court said that it was untenable to claim to retain title to something which no longer existed.

In *Re Bond Worth Ltd,.* known as the Monsanto case, the seller had attempted to impose a condition in its contract retaining 'equitable and beneficial' ownership of Acrilan which it had sold for use in the process of making man-made fibre. Monsanto, the seller, lost the case because the judge held that the clause did not give it any legal ownership — which, he said, had passed on delivery of the Acrilan. He said Monsanto had an equitable interest capable of being registered at Companies House under Companies Act 1948, Section 95 but, as it had not been so registered, he held that Monsanto had no priority over other creditors and was totally unsecured.

The lessons to be learned from these major cases are varied. To be effective, a retention of title clause must specifically retain legal ownership. Sellers seeking to protect themselves will run into substantial difficulties where what is being sold is to be used in a manufacturing process, rather than resold in the same (or similar) form. Buyers seeking credit of whatever kind from external sources must be prepared to disclose their contracts to potential lenders who will need to be satisfied that the debtor does in fact own what it is offering as security. Above all, traders must understand the wording and effect of the contracts which they make. In both the Borden and Monsanto cases the clauses were held to be ineffective. Simply because a contract contains certain terms they are not necessarily effective, binding or sacrosanct.

Consideration must also be given to the question of insurance, which is primarily concerned with risk rather than ownership. In two of the above cases risk was expressed to pass on delivery, which is the normal rule under the Sale of Goods Act 1893, and so the buyer, though not owning the goods, had an insurable interest. In the event of a company failing, or a receiver being appointed, loss or damage to goods subject to a valid retention of title clause could constitute a double burden in the absence of adequate insurance.

In the opinion of *True and Fair*, the statement on auditing, 'Guidance for auditors on the implications of goods sold subject to reservation of title', is still relevant. However, clients should review the type of clauses incorporated in their conditions of sale in the light of the Monsanto and Scottish Timber decisions. From an audit point of view, every reservation clause should be subjected to critical examination.

# 16  *Management Representations*

*There are certain perennial audit problems and procedures, and in early 1982 the Auditing Practices Committee issued a draft guideline on Management Representations.*

*The letter of representation was itself given greater significance by the Companies Act 1976 in an indirect way: it made it a criminal offence for directors to mislead the auditors, even though there is no intention to deceive (i.e. if they do so recklessly), and irrespective of whether the representation is given orally or in writing.*

*The following is the text of the 1982 Guideline. (The italic emphasis has been added to highlight those sections which are different from previous professional recommendations.)*

## Introduction

1. Paragraph 4 of the Auditing Standard 'The auditor's operational standard' states: 'the auditor should obtain relevant and reliable audit evidence sufficient to enable him to draw reasonable conclusions therefrom'. This evidence will be obtained from many different sources. Representations from management are one such source.

2. Oral representations will be made throughout the audit in response to specific enquiries. Whilst management representations constitute valid audit evidence, the auditor should not, in respect of any significant aspect of the audit, rely solely on unsupported oral representations of management as being sufficient reliable evidence. Most representations can be corroborated by checking with sources independent of the enterprise or by checking with evidence generated by the auditor. Where adequate corroboration is not and could not reasonably be expected to be available, the auditor should ensure that there is no other evidence which conflicts with the representations made by management and that the representations are confirmed in writing. *Such written representations should be confined to matters which are material to the financial statements and which are mainly considerations affecting judgement and opinion. Matters of fact can also be included, however, where they are material and where knowledge of the fact is confined to management.*

3. Having obtained written representations, the auditor must still decide whether in the circumstances, these representations together with such other audit evidence as he has obtained are sufficient to enable him to form an unqualified opinion on the financial statements.

4. As a secondary consideration, the formal recording of management's views and judgements on essential matters also serves to emphasise that responsibility for those views and judgements rests with management.

## Procedures

5. *A summary of representations made by management to the auditor in respect of material matters should be prepared at the conclusion of the audit. The auditor should ensure that these representations are either formally minuted as being approved by the board of directors or included in a signed letter, known as a 'letter of representation'.*

6. Because the representations are those of management, the latter should be encouraged to participate in drafting any letter of representation or, after review and discussion, to make

appropriate amendments to the auditor's draft, provided that the value of the audit evidence obtained is not thereby diminished. Any letter of representation should be addressed to the auditor and should preferably be prepared on the enterprise's notepaper.

7. Any letter of representation should be signed by persons whose level of authority is appropriate to the significance of the representations made — normally by one or more of the executive directors (for example by the chief executive and the chief financial officer), on behalf of the whole board. The signatories of the letter should also be fully conversant with the matters contained in it. The auditor should request that the consideration of the letter and its approval by the board for signature be minuted.

8. If procedures regarding management representations have been agreed beforehand, the auditor is unlikely to be faced with a refusal by the management to cooperate in providing such representations. *However, management may, at the outset, indicate that they are not willing to sign formal letters of representation or to pass minutes requested by the auditor. If they do so indicate, the auditor should inform management that he will himself prepare a statement in writing setting out his understanding of the principal representations that they have made to him during the course of the audit and he should send this statement to them with a request for a confirmation that his understanding of the representations is correct. If management disagree with the auditor's statement of representations, discussions should be held to clarify the matters in doubt, and if necessary a revised statement prepared and agreed. Should management fail to reply, the auditor should follow the matter up to try to ensure that his understanding of the position, as set out in his statement, is correct. If he is unable to satisfy himself, even after discussion with management of their oral representations, the auditor may have to conclude that the has not received all the information and explanations that he requires, and he will then need to consider qualifying his audit report to this effect on the grounds of limitation in the scope of his audit procedures.*

## Dating

9. *The formal record of management representations should be dated as close as possible to the date of the audit report and after all other work, including the post balance sheet events review, has been completed. It should never be dated after the audit report since it is part of the evidence on which the auditor's opinion expressed in his report is based.* If there is a substantial delay between the date of the formal representations and the date of the audit report, the auditor should consider whether to obtain further representations in respect of the intervening period and also consider whether any additional audit procedures need to be carried out, as described in the Auditing Guideline *Events after the Balance Sheet Date.*

## Contents and Wording

10. The precise scope of formal management representations should be appropriate to the circumstances of each particular audit and confined to matters which are material to the financial statements, as indicated in Paragraph 2 above. Set out in Appendix 1 is a list of areas in respect of which the auditor might consider the need for management representations. *Attached as Appendix 2 is an example of a letter of representation illustrating the need to confine management representations to material matters.*

## Appendix 1   Possible Areas for Management Representations

Set out below is a list of possible areas in respect of which the auditor might consider the need for management representations. The precise scope of such representations should be appropriate to the circumstances of the particular audit and should be confined to material matters.

*General*
  (a) all transactions properly recorded in the accounting records;
  (b) all financial records and related data, including minutes of management and shareholder meetings, made available to the auditor;
  (c) value and classification of assets and liabilities in the financial statements not materially affected by management's plans and intentions (especially relevant if closures or sales of segments of the enterprise and planned).

*Assets*
  Fixed
    (a) title to assets;
    (b) disclosure of all charges on assets;
    (c) adequacy and consistency of depreciation;
    (d) write off of assets sold and scrapped.
  Stocks
    (a) valuation at lower of cost and net realisable value;
    (b) quantity established by physical count;
    (c) long-term contract work in progress stated at cost plus attributable profit, less foreseeable losses;
    (d) all stocks and completed orders which have been invoiced to customers excluded from year end stocks in balance sheet.
  Investments
    (a) disclosure of holdings over 10%;
    (b) reasonable valuation, if based on directors' estimates.
  Debtors
    full (but not excessive) provision for doubtful and bad debts.
  Cash
    all bank and cash balances included in the balance sheet.
  Other current
    all other current assets expected to realise at least amounts at which stated.

*Liabilities*
  (a) all known liabilities included in the accounts and sufficient, but not excessive, provision made for estimated liabilities;
  (b) adequacy of provision for tax payable on unrealised gains and timing differences, unless noted as a contingency.

*Contingencies*
  (a) tax liabilities (including deferred tax) not provided for;
  (b) unfunded pension payments not provided for;
  (c) guarantees and warranties, including those on behalf of subsidiaries and associates;
  (d) bills discounted;
  (e) debts factored with recourse.

*Legal claims*
  (a) from customers, for faulty goods;
  (b) from employees, for unfair dismissal or injury;
  (c) involving other parties which are outstanding.

*Future commitments*
  (a) to buy fixed assets and investments (separate disclosure of expenditure approved and contracted for, and approved and not contracted for);
  (b) to borrow or lend money;
  (c) to buy stock in excess of normal requirements or prevailing prices;
  (d) to acquire shares under options or loan conversion rights.

*Profit and loss account*
  Disclosure of
    (a) unusual transactions;
    (b) prior year items.

## Other matters

(a) disclosure or adjustment, as appropriate, of significant post balance sheet events;

(b) disclosure of directors' interests in contracts or transactions with the company as required by statute;

(c) details of transactions conducted with other related parties other than at arms length, e.g. connected persons and affiliated companies under common control;

(d) adequacy of working capital to meet foreseeable requirements for next 12 months;

(e) reasons for changes in accounting policies;

(f) appropriateness of indices used in current cost financial statements;

(g) realistic expectation of useful lives of fixed assets included in current cost financial statements.


## Appendix 2   An Example of a Letter of Representation

Dear Sirs,

We confirm the following information given to you in connection with your audit of the company's financial statements for the year ended . . . in accordance with the requirements of the Companies Acts 1948 to 1981.

### General

To the best of our knowledge and belief all transactions undertaken by the company have been properly recorded in the accounting records and all financial records and related data, including minutes of management and shareholders' meetings, have been made available to you.

All known assets and liabilities as at the balance sheet date have been included in the financial statements. Their value and classification are not materially affected by any management plans.

### Slow Moving Stocks

Having carefully reviewed calculations of net realisable values of slow moving stocks estimated at £1,000,000 at . . . together with the progress of the selling programme since that date, we are of the opinion that the realisations from the remaining slow moving stocks will be sufficient, after allowing for expenses expected to be incurred in respect of their disposal, to produce the amount included in the financial statements as their aggregate net realisable value at that date.

### Balance due from XYZ Ltd.

The amount of £1,500,000 due from XYZ Ltd., an associated company, has been outstanding since . . . but is in our opinion fully recoverable and consequently no provision is required against this balance.

### Deferred Taxation

The board considers that its present commitments to capital expenditure, together with its plans for future development, strongly indicate that the benefit of timing differences attributable to first year allowances will be retained in the foreseeable future. When assessing the probability that timing differences in respect of accelerated capital allowances will not reverse, the board considered and reviewed the latest management estimates of capital expenditure. Therefore, no provision for deferred taxation is required in respect of these timing differences.

### Contingencies and Post-Balance Sheet Events

(a) There is no pending litigation either in the hands of the company's solicitors or otherwise and there were no contingent liabilities of a material amount for which provision has not been made in the financial statements other than as noted.

(b) There have, to the best of our knowledge and belief, been no events since the date of the balance sheet which necessitate any revision of the figures included in the financial statements or any addition to the notes thereto.

*Profit and Loss Account*

Except as disclosed in the financial statements, the results for the year were not materially affected by:

(a) transactions of a sort not usually undertaken by the company;
(b) circumstances of an exceptional or non-recurrent nature;
(c) charges or credits relating to prior periods; or
(d) any change in accounting policies.

*Current Cost Financial Statements*

The indices used in the current cost financial statements for the year ended . . . are, in our opinion, appropriate to the business of the company and have been applied on a proper basis to assets and liabilities. The expected useful lives of fixed assets have been estimated on a realistic basis after taking into account their current age and expected technological changes.

Yours faithfully,

# 17    The Audit of Post-Balance Sheet Events

*One of the most popular examination topics has always been the significance of post-balance sheet events and the Accounting Standards Committee has produced a standard on this subject in the form of SSAP 17. Many firms regard post-balance sheet verification work as of such importance that specific programmes are designed to ensure that the post-balance sheet period is utilised fully. The note which follows reminds students of the circumstances in which post-balance sheet events should be taken into account, and outlines a suitable audit programme.*

## Background

Current auditing examination questions often concern what we might call *audit management*, a subject to which professional practices are paying increasing attention. In its fullest sense this covers a substantial range of matter, including the use of checklists, standardisation of working schedules, questionnaires, systems documentation, confirmation, letters and reports, sampling and review procedures, as well as the organised training, which necessarily accompanies the above. In essence, the phrase 'audit management' encapsulates the art of performing an audit.

(a) *conscientiously*, without material omission, and hence with minimum risk of liability;
(b) *profitably*; and
(c) as *rapidly* as is compatible with (a) and (b) above, so as not to cause any delay in the presentation of accounts to shareholders.

Elaborating on the latter objective, although it is generally accepted that the earliest possible publication of the accounts materially enhances their value to all interested parties, there is a certain conflict which should not be overlooked: this lies in the extraordinary usefulness to the auditor of the period between the balance sheet date and the signing of the accounts. Events which take place during this period may be highly instructive as to the true position at the end of the financial period in question, and a shortening of this period may therefore be correspondingly disadvantageous from the point of view of accuracy.

While auditors have to bow to the demand for speed in producing accounts (as now reflected in the heavy penalties for late filing prescribed in the Companies Act 1976), there is nevertheless a good deal which they can do to optimise the usefulness of the (albeit shortened) post-balance sheet period; indeed a number of firms have now incorporated a specific *subsequent events programme* within the scope of their prescribed audit procedures.

The ICAEW Research Committee has produced an 'occasional paper' on this subject and the ASC has produced SSAP 17, on which the APC sought Counsel's opinion before issuing its own Guideline for auditors; while in the USA it provides the subject matter of their first Statement on Auditing Standards (SAS 1). One of the most straightforward and authoritative statements on this matter, however, is Institute Statement N 17, issued nearly 20 years ago. Its basic message was simple and it still applies: events taking place after the financial period has ended should be disregarded unless (a) they relate to legislative change which requires reflection in the accounts retrospectively, such as new disclosure requirements, or a change in corporation tax rate affecting charges for future taxation; or (b) they tell us something about the company's *true* position on the balance sheet date which, on that date, was not known either at all or with any degree of certainty.

Examples of (b) will readily be appreciated in those events which either confirm or allay doubts concerning bad debt provisions, pending litigation, and contingent liabilities. In every such case an event *within* the period under review raises the doubts; the *subsequent* event merely informs us of the outcome or materially increases our knowledge of what the outcome is most likely to be.

Certain post-balance sheet happenings will require particular care, such as a fall in the realisable value of stocks of certain finished goods as a result of which incurred overheads (incorporated in the balance sheet values of those goods) may not be recovered. In such a case a thorough assessment of the circumstances and cause of the fall must be made to determine in which accounting period the likely loss should be reflected.

## The 'Subsequent Events' Audit Programme

In order to make optimum use of the post-balance sheet period it is preferable that a formal but flexible, *written programme* be used rather than the haphazard approach of leaving matters to the intuition of the audit clerks (an attribute for which, generally, there are not famous). Such a standard programme should be divided into *four* stages, and would normally commence with the rather obvious tests of *year-end cut-off arrangements*; these tests would ensure — on the evidence of (a) subsequently recorded book entries, (b) independently received documents (from customers and suppliers), and (c) movements of goods in and out of stores — that balance sheet quantities had been determined on a valid basis, consistent with that used for arriving at purchases and sales respectively.

*Stage two* comprises a *comparison of business activity levels* before and after the year end. Normally this comparison would focus on the monthly totals for sales, purchases, receipts and payments and, if available, would also include the results of operations. Any unexplained material discrepancies would be thoroughly investigated.

The *third stage* involves *formal discussions* with senior executives of the client company (during which full notes must be taken) on a wide range of post-balance sheet matters, including: (a) current market conditions, the effect of new products and changes in competition; (b) changes in selling prices of company products; (c) significant variations in production and other costs; (d) subsequent bookings/cancellations of sales orders, and losses of major customers; (e) capital expenditure commitments; (f) new borrowings and share or loan issues, (g) liabilities (e.g. guarantees) in dispute and pending lawsuits; and (h) changes in accounting and financial policy. Minutes of all post-balance sheet board meetings would be carefully examined in the course of this stage.

The *final stage* of the programme involves a *thorough review* of findings to date, so that decisions may be reached on any necessary adjustments in the light of subsequent events, and these should be discussed in detail with the directors.

It should be stressed that the above is little more than an outline of the enquiries which may lead to adjustment of the draft accounts. Its adaptation to meet the particular situation is therefore essential.

## SSAP 17 — Accounting for Post-Balance Sheet Events

*Part 1 — Explanatory Note*

1. Events arising after the balance sheet date need to be reflected in financial statements if they provide additional evidence of conditions that existed at the balance sheet date and materially affect the amounts to be included.

2. To prevent financial statements from being misleading, disclosure needs to be made by way of notes of other material events arising after the balance sheet date which provide evidence of conditions not existing at the balance sheet date. Disclosure is required where this information is necessary for a proper understanding of the financial position.

3. A post balance sheet event for the purpose of this standard is an event which occurs between the balance sheet date and the date on which the financial statements are approved by the board of directors. It is not intended that the preliminary consideration of a matter which may lead to a decision by the board of directors in the future should fall within the scope of this standard.

4. Events which occur after the date on which the financial statements are approved by the board of directors do not come within the scope of this standard. If such events are material the directors should consider publishing the relevant information so that users of financial statements are not misled.

5. The process involved in the approval of financial statements by the directors will vary depending on the management structure and procedures followed in preparing and finalising financial statements. However, the date of approval will normally be the date of the board meeting at which the financial statements are formally approved, or in respect of unincorporated enterprises the corresponding date. In respect of group accounts, the date of approval is the date the group accounts are formally approved by the board of directors of the holding company.

*Classification of post balance sheet events*

6. Events occurring after the balance sheet date may be classified into two categories: 'adjusting events' and 'non-adjusting events'.

7. Adjusting events are events which provide additional evidence relating to conditions existing at the balance sheet date. They require changes in amounts to be included in financial statements. Examples of adjusting events are given in the appendix.

8. Some events occurring after the balance sheet date, such as a deterioration in the operating results and in the financial position, may indicate a need to consider whether it is appropriate to use the going concern concept in the preparation of financial statements. Consequently these may fall to be treated as adjusting events.

9. Non-adjusting events are events which arise after the balance sheet date and concern conditions which did not exist at that time. Consequently they do not result in changes in amounts in financial statements. They may, however, be of such materiality that their disclosure is required by way of notes to ensure that financial statements are not misleading. Examples of non-adjusting events which may require disclosure are given in the appendix.

10 .Disclosure would be required of the reversal or maturity after the year end of transactions entered into before the year end, the substance of which was primarily to alter the appearance of the company's balance sheet. Such alterations include those commonly known as 'window dressing'.

11. There are certain post balance sheet events which, because of statutory requirements or customary accounting practice, are reflected in financial statements and so fall to be treated as adjusting events. These include proposed dividends, amounts appropriated to reserves, the effects of changes in taxation and dividends receivable from subsidiary and associated companies.

*Disclosure in financial statements*

12. Separate disclosure of adjusting events is not normally required as they do no more than provide additional evidence in support of items in financial statements.

13. In determining which non-adjusting events are of sufficient materiality to require disclosure, regard should be had to all matters which are necessary to enable users of financial statements to assess the financial position.

*Part 2 — Definition of Terms*

14. *Financial statements* are balance sheets, profit and loss accounts, statements of source and application of funds, notes and other statements, which collectively are intended to give a true and fair view of financial position and profit or loss.

15. *Company* includes any enterprise which comes within the scope of statements of standard accounting practice.

16. *Directors* include the corresponding officers of organisations which do not have directors.

17. *The date on which the financial statements are approved by the board of directors* is the date the board of directors formally approves a set of documents as the financial statements. In respect of unincorporated enterprises, the date of approval is the corresponding date. In respect of group accounts, the date of approval is the date when the group accounts are formally approved by the board of directors of the holding company.

18. *Post-balance sheet events* are those events, both favourable and unfavourable, which occur between the balance sheet date and the date on which the financial statements are approved by the board of directors.

19. *Adjusting events* are post-balance sheet events which provide additional evidence of conditions existing at the balance sheet date. They include events which because of statutory or conventional requirements are reflected in financial statements.

20. *Non-adjusting events* are post balance sheet events which concern conditions which did not exist at the balance sheet date.

## Part 3 — Standard Accounting Practice

21. Financial statements should be prepared on the basis of conditions existing at the balance sheet date.

22. A material post balance sheet event requires changes in the amounts to be included in financial statements where:

(a) it is an adjusting event; or
(b) it indicates that application of the going concern concept to the whole or a material part of the company is not appropriate.

23. A material post-balance sheet event should be disclosed where:

(a) it is a non-adjusting event of such materiality that its non-disclosure would affect the ability of the users of financial statements to reach a proper understanding of the financial position; or
(b) it is the reversal or maturity after the year end of a transaction entered into before the year end, the substance of which was primarily to alter the appearance of the company's balance sheet.

24. In respect of each post balance sheet event which is required to be disclosed under paragraph 23 above, the following information should be stated by way of notes in financial statements:

(a) the nature of the event; and
(b) an estimate of the financial effect, or a statement that it is not practicable to make such an estimate.

25. The estimate of the financial effect should be disclosed before taking account of taxation, and the taxation implications should be explained where necessary for a proper understanding of the financial position.

26. The date on which the financial statements are approved by the board of directors should be disclosed in the financial statements.

## Appendix

*This appendix is for general guidance and does not form part of the statement of standard accounting practice. The examples are merely illustrative and the lists are not exhaustive.*

The examples listed distinguish between those normally classified as adjusting events and as non-adjusting events. However, in exceptional circumstances, to accord with the prudence concept, an adverse event which would normally be classified as non-adjusting may need to be reclassified as adjusting. In such circumstances, full disclosure of the adjustment would be required.

*Adjusting Events*

The following are examples of post balance sheet events which normally should be classified as adjusting events:

(a) *Fixed assets*. The subsequent determination of the purchase price or of the proceeds of sale of assets purchased or sold before the year end.

(b) *Property*. A valuation which provides evidence of a permanent diminution in value.

(c) *Investments*. The receipt of a copy of the financial statements or other information in respect of an unlisted compoany which provides evidence of a permanent diminution in the value of a long-term investment.

(d) *Stocks and work in progress*.
   (i)  The receipt of proceeds of sales after the balance sheet date or other evidence concerning the net realisable value of stocks.
   (ii) The receipt of evidence that the previous estimate of accrued profit on a long-term contract was materially inaccurate.

(e) *Debtors*. The renegotiation of amounts owing by debtors, or the insolvency of a debtor.

(f) *Dividends receivable*. The declaration of dividends by subsidiaries and associated companies relating to periods prior to the balance sheet date of the holding company.

(g) *Taxation*. The receipt of information regarding rates of taxation.

(h) *Claims*. Amounts received or receivable in respect of insurance claims which were in the course of negotiation at the balance sheet date.

(i) *Discoveries*. The discovery of errors or frauds which show that the financial statements were incorrect.

*Non-adjusting Events*

The following are examples of post balance sheet events which normally should be classified as non-adjusting events:

(a) *Mergers* and acquisitions.
(b) *Reconstructions* and proposed reconstructions.
(c) *Issues* of shares and debentures.
(d) *Purchases and sales of fixed assets* and investments.
(e) *Losses of fixed assets* or stocks as a result of a catastrophe such as fire or flood.
(f) *Opening new trading activities* or extending existing trading activities.
(g) *Closing a significant part of the trading activities* if this was not anticipated at the year end.
(h) *Decline in the value* of property and investments held as fixed assets, if it can be demonstrated that the decline occurred after the year end.
(i) *Changes in rates of foreign exchange*.
(j) *Government action*, such as nationalisation.
(k) *Strikes* and other labour disputes.
(l) *Augmentation of pension benefits*.

**General Critical Note**

It is surprising that so must time elapsed before the implementation of a definitive standard on what, after all, must be one of the least controversial of accounting problems. One of the most contentious aspects of SSAP 17, however, undoubtedly lies in its suggestion that 'post-balance sheet events', as defined, are those events which take place between the accounting date and the date on which the directors approve the accounts. This means that anything happening after the latter date would not be classified as a post-balance sheet event — and this suggestion is nothing short of a misguided attempt to change the meaning of words, since *all* events following the accounting date must, by definition, be post-balance sheet events. It is not unduly cynical to suggest that the imposition of a 'backstop' date in this context represents an attempt primarily to curtail the liability of auditors.

The American SAS 1 more sensibly divides the post-balance sheet period between (a) the phase between the accounting date and the date on which the auditors complete their fieldwork — a period of *primary* audit responsibility, to which the usual rules of adjusting and non-adjusting accounting treatment would apply; and (b) the period after the completion of audit fieldwork — a period of *secondary* audit responsibility, during which adjustments would arise only on the basis of information which reaches the auditors' attention. During this phase no active investigative duty is imposed upon them.

Should the issue ever be tested in the courts or in any other arena in which public expectation of auditors may be gauged, it is likely that auditors would be regarded as having a duty to make known to all readers of accounts the effect upon those accounts of all material subsequent events — irrespective of whether those events took place before or after the approval of the accounts by the directors.

## The APC Guideline — Events after the Balance Sheet Date

### Preface

This Guideline is intended to clarify the responsibilities of the auditor for examining and reporting upon events which occur after the date of the balance sheet. It also gives guidance on the dating of the audit report. Counsel's opinion on the dating of audit reports was obtained before the Guideline was developed. Counsel has subsequently confirmed that this Guideline is in accordance with the relevant statutory provisions and legal principles and that he approves it accordingly.

The Guideline is supplementary to and should be read in conjunction with the auditor's operational and reporting standards and related guidelines.

### Introduction

1. Post balance sheet events are defined by Statement of Standard Accounting Practice No. 17 as 'those events, both favourable and unfavourable, which occur between the balance sheet date and the date on which the financial statements are approved by the board of directors'.

### Scope

2. This Guideline is written in the context of the audit of limited companies. The auditor of an enterprise other than a limited company will be guided by the terms of his particular appointment or by relevant legislation. However, in the absence of specific provisions to the contrary, either in legislation or in the auditor's terms of appointment, the general principle holds that the auditor's duty to his client in respect of a particular assignment does not cease until after the date of his report.

### The Dating of the Audit Report

3. The auditor should always date his audit report. The date used should, in principle, be that on which the auditor signs his report on the financial statements. If, for administrative reasons, final copies of the financial statements are not available at the date the auditor declares himself willing to sign his report, he may use that date or a subsequent date before he signs, provided the delay in the preparation of final copies is only of short duration.

4. The auditor's responsibility is to report on the financial statements as presented by the

directors. It follows that the auditor can never date his report earlier than the date at which the complete financial statements were approved by the directors. Before signing his report, the auditor should obtain evidence that the financial statements have been approved by the directors. Statement of Standard Accounting Practice No. 17 requires disclosure of the date on which the directors approved the financial statements.

5. At the date on which the financial statements are approved by the directors, printed or type-written accounts in the form finally submitted to shareholders may not be available. The auditor should satisfy himself that the directors have approved financial statements which are complete in all material respects. Accordingly the financial statements approved by the directors should not leave unresolved any matters which require exercise of judgement or discretion (although they may omit items which merely require mechanical calculation: for example, the provision of a dividend at a rate already agreed by the directors). The financial statements approved by the directors should take account of Companies Acts, Statements of Standard Accounting Practice and other relevant requirements.

## Events up to the Date of the Audit Report

6. The auditor has a duty to take reasonable steps, as identified in Para. 13, to ensure that he is aware of all significant events up to the date of his report.

He should ensure that any such significant events are, where appropriate, accounted for or disclosed in the financial statements. If not, he should consider whether to qualify his report.

## Events after the Date of the Audit Report

7. After the date of the audit report and before the general meeting at which the financial statements are laid before the members, the auditor does not have a duty actively to search for evidence of post balance sheet events. However, if he becomes aware of information, from sources either within or outside the company, which might have led him to give a different audit opinion, had he possessed the information at the date of his report, he should discuss the matter with the directors. He should then consider whether the financial statements should be amended.

If the directors are unwilling to take action which the auditor considers necessary to inform the shareholders of the changed situation, the auditor should consider exercising his rights under Section 14(7) of the Companies Act 1967 to make a statement at the general meeting at which the financial statements are laid before the members. He should also consider taking legal advice on his position. The auditor does not have a right to communicate directly in writing with shareholders except when he wishes to resign or where it is proposed to remove him.

8. If the directors wish to amend the previously approved financial statements after the auditor has signed his report but before they have been sent to the shareholders, the auditor will need to consider whether the proposed amendments affect his report. His report, revised if necessary, should not be dated before the date on which the amended financial statements are approved by the directors. The auditor's duties, as referred to in Para. 6 above, will need to be extended to the date of his report on the amended financial statements.

9. If the directors wish to amend the financial statements after they have been sent to shareholders and substitute amended ones for approval at the general meeting, the auditor should make a report on the amended financial statements. In this latter report he should refer to the original financial statements and his report on them.

10. After the general meeting at which the financial statements are laid before the members, the auditor has no duty to consider the effect of further subsequent events on the financial statements laid before that meeting. However, if he becomes aware of any events which he considers do materially affect those financial statements he should inform the directors. He should also consider taking legal advice on his position.

*Procedures for the Audit of Post Balance Sheet Events*

11. Certain events and transactions occurring after the balance sheet date are examined by the auditor as part of his normal verification work on the balance sheet. For example, he may check cash received from certain debtors or the amounts realised from the sale of stock after the year end. In addition, the auditor should carry out procedures which are generally known collectively as a Post-Balance Sheet Events review.

12. The objective of the review is to obtain reasonable assurance that all material post balance sheet events, including window dressing transactions, have been identified and, where appropriate, either disclosed or accounted for in the financial statements.

13. The review should consist of discussions with management relating to, and may also include examination of:

(a) the accounting records and any management accounts;

(b) profit forecasts and cash flow projections, or informal estimates made by management;

(c) known 'risk' areas and contingencies whether inherent in the nature of the business (e.g. price fluctuations in commodities) or revealed by previous audit experience;

(d) minutes of shareholders', directors' and management meetings, and correspondence and memoranda relating to items included in the minutes,

(e) relevant information from sources outside the enterprise and public knowledge of other enterprises especially competitors, suppliers and customers, which may come to his attention.

This review should be updated to a date as near as practicable to that of the audit report by making enquiries of management and considering the need to carry out further tests.

*Contingencies*

14. As part of his review of post balance sheet events, the auditor should consider the existence of contingencies and their treatment in the financial statements. Statement of Standard Accounting Practice No 18 — *Accounting for Contingencies* — requires the disclosure of material contingent losses, except where the possibility of loss is remote, and of material contingent gains only if it is probable that the gain will be realised. The auditor will need to use his judgement in determining 'remoteness' and probability' in individual cases. He should pay particular regard to the different treatment required by the Standard, on grounds of prudence, for contingent gains on the one hand and contingent losses on the other.

*Management representations*

15. The auditor should ensure that the record of the formal representations of management is dated as close as possible to the date of the audit report and after all other work including the review of post balance sheet events has been completed. Where there is a substantial delay between the date of the formal representations of management and the date of the audit report, the auditor should consider whether to obtain further written representations in respect of the intervening period.

16. The formal representations or further representations of management should include confirmation of events which have occurred since the balance sheet date and which have had or may have a material effect on the financial position of the enterprise. The record of such representations should refer to any significant legal actions that are outstanding. Also, where in the directors' opinion, no events have occurred since the balance sheet date which have had, or may have, a material effect on the financial position of the enterprise, this opinion should be included in the formal representations or further representations of management.

*Working papers*

17. The working papers should contain a record of the work carried out to identify post balance sheet events. Where discussions have taken place with the management regarding matters arising from the review of post balance sheet events, a note of the discussions should be retained by the auditor.

*Groups*

18. When the post balance sheet review is made in respect of consolidated financial statements, the auditor of the holding company will need to have regard to the work carried out in this area by the auditors of subsidiaries. In normal circumstances, audited financial statements of the subsidiaries will be available to him at the time he signs his report on the consolidated financial statements, and the auditors of the subsidiaries will have carried out a review of the post balance sheet events up to the date of their reports. The auditor of the holding company will need to ensure that he carries out appropriate procedures to identify post balance sheet events of significance to the group between the dates of the reports of the auditors of subsidiaries and the date of his own report.

# 18 Auditing Deferred Taxation

*This section relates to the substitution of SSAP 15 for the withdrawn SSAP 11 on deferred taxation, and highlights the audit implications which arise in view of the inherent subjectivity of many of the decisions which have to be made on deferred taxation. The notes which follow should be read in conjunction with the SSAP 15 'checklist' at the end of this text.*

**Audit Implications of SSAP 15**

*Introduction*

When SSAP 11 was passed as a Standard, it appears that the full impact on amounts set aside for deferred taxation was not fully appreciated. The causes of the problem lay in

(a) the effect of substantial price increases on the amount of balancing charges arising on asset replacement;
(b) stock relief for corporation tax purposes;
(c) capital gains rolling-over provisions resulting in the deferment of corporation tax while the business or division involved remained a going concern.

As a result of the above very large amounts of deferred taxation were set aside — not to be included as part of shareholders' funds — but which, at the same time, were extremely unlikely ever to result in the actual payment to the Revenue of a taxation liability.

Due to the resistance and resentment generated by this situation, SSAP 11 was withdrawn by the ASC and SSAP 15 has now been substituted.

Curiously, following the issue of SSAP 15 the economic tide turned once again, and it was recognised that many of the tax allowances (e.g. stock appreciation, asset replacement) required financial resources which, in a recession, are beyond those available to many companies, and only a change in the 'clawback' rules in 1980 prevented a reversion back to the full deferred tax provisions of the replaced SSAP 11!

*Audit Implications*

SSAP 15, *Accounting for Deferred Taxation*, introduced new areas of judgement and assessment of probabilities for the auditor. Its main requirements are

(a) deferred tax should be accounted for by the liability method in respect of the tax reduction arising from all originating timing differences of material amount, including stock appreciation relief;
(b) if a company can *demonstrate* with *reasonable probability* that any tax reduction will continue for the *foreseeable future*, deferred taxation need not be provided for within the profit and loss account;
(c) the potential amount of deferred tax on all timing differences should be disclosed by way of notes to the accounts;
(d) deferred tax should not be shown as part of shareholders' funds.

*Critical Audit Factors*

The critical audit points in the new approach are:

(a) it is up to the company to demonstrate that a deferred tax provision is not required;

(b) there must be a reasonable probability that tax reductions will continue;

(c) the period for consideration is the 'foreseeable' future.

If there is real doubt as to whether tax will or will not be payable, then provision for deferred tax should be made.

The existence of material unutilised capital allowances at the balance sheet date will usually mean that the company does not have to demonstrate to the auditor as much in the way of future expenditure intentions and availability of finance as will be the case where no backlog of unutilised allowance exists.

### The Need to Examine Budgets

In other instances, the pattern of past capital expenditure and stock investment may mean that the auditor will not need to rely solely on future projections. Differing circumstances, therefore, will probably require companies to provide differing degrees of supporting documentation for auditors. However, it may be necessary (particularly where no backlog of unutilised allowances exists, or where no consistent pattern of expenditure can be shown from past experience) for a *company to prepare*, and for the *auditor to examine*, a series of budgets in respect of

(a) the trading position showing estimated profit and the depreciation charge;

(b) a cash flow budget;

(c) a capital expenditure and disposals budget;

(d) a forecast of stock values.

A company which does not provide these statements may well find it difficult to convince its auditor that a deferred tax provision is not required.

### 'Reasonable Probability'

After examining all available evidence (including the company's past level of success in forecasting) the auditor must decide whether a deferred tax provision is necessary or not. A 50 : 50 chance of success, on the one hand, would be too low and absolute certainty, on the other, impossible to achieve. Auditors will therefore need to judge which types of timing difference in a company are likely to be most susceptible to variation from the forecast level. For example, in some cases the degree of probability of obtaining stock relief may, given the risk of supply shortages, be less than that of being able to incur the requisite level of capital expenditure. The degree of certainty required will then depend upon the materiality of the amounts involved in the context of all other factors affecting a company's future.

### 'Foreseeable Future'

This term is itself a subjective one and the Standard does not include a definition. However, in order to provide some assurance that provisions for taxation, deferred or current, are not created or released at frequent intervals and in the wrong accounting periods, it is necessary to forecast the relevant factors, and it may be thought that a period of some three years is suitable in this context.

### Land and Buildings

Deferred taxation on revaluation surpluses on land and buildings will generally no longer be necessary, but as soon as the directors have taken a decision to dispose of the property and not to re-invest the proceeds to obtain roll over relief, a provision should be made.

## Conclusion

In order that auditors can form a view as to the general applicability of the provisions of SSAP 15, they will need to consider, in the light of their everyday experience, the following questions:

(a) how far ahead in time should forecasts extend, whether documented or not?
(b) to the extent that forecasts do need to be documented, what degree of supporting evidence will be needed, and is such information likely to be available?
(c) what, in practical terms, constitutes 'reasonable probability'?

## General Notes

*Presentation of the deferred taxation note.*   Where the tax effect of timing differences, due both to the excess of tax allowances over depreciation and to stock appreciation relief that cannot be demonstrated with reasonable probability to continue in the future, is entirely offset by the tax effect of trading losses carried forward, a suggested presentation of the deferred taxation note is as shown in Table 3.

A note to the financial statements should indicate the extent to which the taxation charge for the period has been reduced both by timing differences on which deferred taxation has not been provided in accordance with the accounting policy, and by the utilisation of tax losses brought forward. The note should also indicate both the extent of those trading losses that have been carried forward to be offset against the taxation liability of future years, and the extent to which those trading losses have been utilised to reduce the amount provided for deferred taxation.

*The effect of the economic climate.*   It is of some interest to note that attempts over the past few years to establish a standard accounting treatment on deferred taxation appear to have reflected inversely the country's economic situation. The first Standard, SSAP 11, on this subject was drafted furing the aftermath of the recession of the early/mid-seventies, and was regarded as suitably restrictive in its import. During the latter years of the decade, with the improvement in corporate profitability, it was felt that substantial sums of what were, in effect, shareholders' funds, were being locked in the deferred taxation provision despite the fact that these sums were unlikely ever to result in the payment to the Revenue of a corporation tax liability. For this reason, SSAP 11 was withdrawn and replaced by the more liberally drafted SSAP 15, now in force.

The latest Standard incorporates phraseology of extraordinary vagueness — 'foreseeable future' and 'reasonable probability', in particular. At the time of writing, the current economic recession (which threatens to be a good deal more severe than its predecessor) is deepening, and the level of corporate bankruptcy is rising sharply; inflation and interest rates are running at effective rates of around 8% and 13% respectively; foreign competition and the weakness of the pound (in spite of North Sea oil) are undermining industrial performance; and the unemployment figures are the highest they have been since the thirties. In such circumstances a realistic application of SSAP 15 terminology is virtually impossible and many auditors must now be

**Table 3**

| | Amount provided (£1000) | Total potential liability (£1000) |
|---|---|---|
| Tax effect of timing differences due to: | | |
| Excess of tax allowances over depreciation | 2,200 | 4,600 |
| Stock appreciation relief | 400 | 4,300 |
| Trading losses | (2,600) | (4,900) |
| Total | — | 4,000 |

acknowledging the possibility that SSAP 11 might have been a more appropriate Standard at the present time, for all its restrictiveness!

Current indications are that the private sector is in for a further squeeze. The renewed deterioration of both the financial position and the profitability of companies may force companies to cut back both their operations and their investment programmes. Under the present tax system, such cut backs may result in an increased tax liability as a result of the clawback of stock relief and the reversal of timing differences on fixed assets.

Before SSAP 15 was introduced, most companies provided deferred taxation in full. By doing this, they could meet out of the deferred tax account any increase in the tax liability that might result from the reversal of timing differences. However, once a company has adopted the provisions of SSAP 15 and has ceased to provide deferred taxation in full, the reversal of timing differences on which deferred taxation has not been provided will result in an abnormally high tax charge in that year's profit and loss account.

Therefore, in the current economic climate, auditors should consider very carefully whether timing differences will reverse in the future. Assumptions that were reasonable in previous years might no longer be valid.

# 19  Risk-Based Auditing

'Risk-based auditing' is the phrase recently coined to cover the present search for an audit approach which reconciles the apparently irreconcilable objectives of (a) minimising professional risk, while (b) guaranteeing full fee recovery on every assignment. The risk-based approach is therefore designed to avoid over-auditing in low complexity (and hence low risk) situations, and under-auditing in high complexity situations respectively.

When asked to elaborate on the researches and field tests currently in progress, technical partners ofter refer to the 80 : 20 statistical norm applicable to most data fields. While not mathematically inevitable, this is a generally observable phenomenon: for example, it has been ascertained that of the one billion cinema tickets sold each year in the USA, 80% are bought by those in the 12 to 24 age group, that is by 20% of the population; a useful piece of marketing data, to say the least!

The equivalent auditing observation is that 80% of audit work is of the 'nuts and bolts' routine variety, and accounts for no more than 20% of the risks; current research is therefore aimed at devising coherent and readily understood systems which enable lower grade (i.e. lower cost) staff to deal with the bulk of the work involving minimal exposure, thereby releasing partners and others on high charge-out rates to concentrate on the judgemental areas which conversely account for 80% of audit risks (such as the adequacy of provisions) and form the basis of most litigious matter, whether or not eventually settled by the courts.

Risk-based auditing distinguishes clearly between transaction testing routines and the testing of account balances. The latter are in turn subdivided so as to identify (a) high-risk and error-prone conditions, which conscientious auditors would require to be covered by a provision; (b) high-value items, where even a small percentage error would be material; and (c) the balances which remain after conditions (a) and (b) are removed, and which therefore require to be tested at an appropriate level. It is in this particular area that the main thrust of research is currently being directed.

This audit approach is best illustrated by reference to Figure 1. Under Condition 1, internal control is known to be reliable; overall reasonableness has been satisfactorily assessed; and the necessary level of assurance is therefore obtained by 'minimum testing', as shown.

Under Condition 2, *either* internal control is reliable *or* overall reasonableness has been satisfactorily assessed. 'More testing' is obviously needed in order to provide the necessary level of assurance.

Under Condition 3, reliance on internal control is either unjustified or uneconomical; assessment of overall reasonableness is either impracticable or shows unsatisfactory results; and the necessary assurance has therefore to be obtained by 'maximum testing', as shown.

The question which inevitably arises relates to the materiality criteria which are used to distinguish high and low value balances respectively. A suitable base, such as total revenue or total assets, must therefore be selected, to which a percentage is then applied to arrive at the appropriate materiality limit. The size of the chosen base determines the percentage to be used, and this percentage will normally fall as the size of the base increases. One firm uses 5% for bases below £25,000, and 0.5% for bases in excess of £8 million, with a sliding scale (subject to the audit partner's discretion) operating in between.

Once the materiality limit is computed on a rational basis, the 'high-value items' shown in Figure 1 are easily identified. The diagram makes it clear, however, that the population of high value items increases in *inverse* proportion to the amount of assurance to be gained from (a) the auditor's assessment of overall reasonableness (based on analytical review of the draft accounts), and (b) his assessment of the internal controls in force.

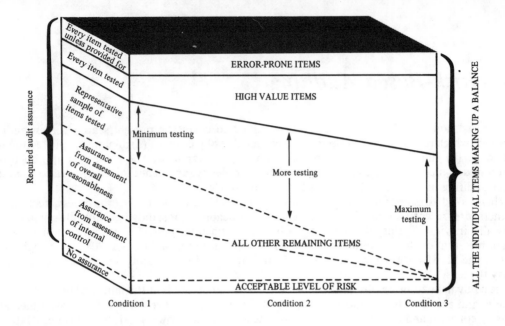

**Figure 1**  Reproduced from TEAM Auditing Systems.


Let us assume, for example, that the procedures already outlined result in a materiality limit of £10,000. If Condition 1 prevails, the materiality limit is divided by 1 (i.e. it remains at £10,000); under Condition 2 it is divided by 2, and all account balances in excess of £5,000 therefore become high-value items; and finally, under Condition 3, by dividing the materiality limit by 3, we see that all balances greater than £3,333 are regarded as high-value items.

The divisors 1, 2 and 3 (known as 'extent factors') correspond with the extent of testing required for risk levels of 37%, 14% and 5% respectively, such risk of course being the failure of audit procedures to detect material error, if it has occurred and remains undetected. (For the technically minded, another way of expressing this is to point out that 1 is the negative natural log (NNL) of 0.37, 2 is the NNL of 0.14, and 3 is the NNL of 0.05.)

Thus, once the error-prone and high-value items are eliminated, the appropriate level of testing the remaining items is easily determined by reference to a 'risk matrix' (as shown in Table 4), it being borne in mind that risk levels are complementary to confidence levels.

From this we see that if an overall confidence level (i.e. audit assurance) of 95% is sought, the sample sizes necessary for the substantive testing of remaining items will be determined by using a confidence level of 63% (the complement of 37% risk) under Condition 1; 86% under Condition 2; and 95% under Condition 3.

The extent of testing which results from applying this system is clearly derived from probability theory, and is based on the principles of 'monetary unit sampling', an attributes sampling technique which is already widely used.

**Table 4**

| | | Condition 1 | Condition 2 | | Condition 3 |
|---|---|---|---|---|---|
| | | Internal control and analytical review satisfactory | Internal control satisfactory | or Analytical review satisfactory | Neither internal control nor analytical review satisfactory |
| | | % risk* | % risk | % risk | % risk |
| Assessing internal control | A | 37 | 37 | 100 | 100 |
| Assessing overall reasonableness | B | 37 | 100 | 37 | 100 |
| Substantively testing balance of remaining items | C | 37 | 14 | 14 | 5 |
| AUDIT RISK (A × B × C) | D | 5 | 5 | 5 | 5 |
| (AUDIT ASSURANCE: 100 – D%) | | (95) | (95) | (95) | (95) |

*The risk is that audit procedures fail to detect material error if it has occurred and remains undetected.

# 20  Mini-computers, Terminals and Microfilm

*The following are brief extract from the relevant sections of the author's book*
Auditing Today *(Prentice-Hall International) on the problems arising from the use of*
*mini-computers to meet the data processing needs of an increasing number of client*
*companies.*

## Mini-computers

The majority of large audit firms now employ staff whose abilities are commensurate with the
tasks imposed by large-scale computer processing. On the other hand, the vast majority of
smaller audit firms are unprepared for the EDP revolution, and it is they who are most likely to
feel the repercussions of their ignorance of modern methods of data processing.

I say this advisedly, particularly in view of the advent of mini-computers which are now well
within the financial reach of all but the smallest of business entities. Many auditors erroneously
regard these streamlined little objects as little more than advanced forms of book-keeping
machines, but nothing could be further from the truth; they are in every sense computers. Indeed,
it could almost be said that their particular attributes render them potentially far more
dangerous, from the security viewpoint, than their large 'main frame' counterparts. These
attributes include

(a) flexibility in application;
(b) adaptability through simple programming;
(c) extremely robust hardware, so that little caution is necessary on the matters of atmospheric
    sensitivity (which, in practice, usually means that the more important fire and flood
    precautions, standby arrangements, etc., are equally ignored — no smoking restrictions,
    for example);
(d) ease of input access, often by terminal;
(e) few technical staff requirements;
(f) visual display unit (VDU) output screens.

As a result, the mini-computer installation is often viewed by staff as being an 'open
house', and all and sundry 'get in on the EDP act'. So simple is its operation that it could,
for an entire processing run, remain under the sole control of one person — an obvious
security hazard. Matters such as controlled access, physical precautions, secrecy of output,
authorisation of program changes, logging of use, care of files, and the innumerable other
security measures, as vital in a mini-computer establishment as in any other, become secondary
considerations and eventually fade entirely. That is, of course, until such neglect results in
the inadvertent destruction of unsupported master files, or a power failure reveals the
deficiency of standby facilities, to mention but two of a range of untoward consequences, of
varying degrees of seriousness for the entity concerned. A mini-computer can all to easily result in
a maxi-disaster!

In such a case it may prove difficult for the auditor, having continuously acquiesced in what
amounts to a flagrant disregard for basic internal control criteria, to establish his own freedom
from culpability in the matter, especially if outside losses result. In short, if this section sounds
like a warning, it is meant to. Liability can no longer be regarded purely in the light of the basic
statutory reporting duty, and data processing methods do not alter principles of law or
established standards of professional competence.

## Problems Arising from the Use of Remote Terminals

Technical innovations have increased the use of remote terminals, usually based upon a VDU and keyboard typewriter, and these have widespread application in commercial organisations. Examples of the use of remote terminals we see in airline booking terminals, bank cash point terminals, and information from branches which can be keyed in on a daily or weekly basis through remote terminals. Such data may relate to current purchases, sales or stock movements.

Many other examples abound, but in each case the chief audit problem arises from the fact that master files held in the central computer store (on discs or drums because of access speed and storage capacity) may be read and updated by remote terminal without an adequate audit trail or, in some cases, any record remaining. Necessary precautions should therefore be made to ensure that these terminals are used in a controlled way, by authorised personnel only.

## Security Techniques

In view of the risks outlined above, a number of recognised techniques have come into general operation in order to control the use of terminals for input purposes. The most important of these techniques include the following:

(a) hardware constraints, e.g. necessitating the use of a key or magnetic-strip badge or card to engage the terminal, or placing the terminal in a location to which access is carefully restricted, and which is constantly monitored by closed-circuit television surveillance systems;

(b) the allocation of identification numbers to authorised terminal operators, with or without the use of passwords; these are checked by the main-frame computer against stored tables of authorised numbers and passwords;

(c) using operator characteristics such as voice prints, hand geometry (finger length ratios) and thumb prints, as a means of identification by the main-frame computer;

(d) restricting the access to particular programs or master files in the main-frame computer, to designated terminals; this arrangement may be combined with those indicated above;

(e) in top-security systems, the authority to allocate authorities such as those indicated above (i.e. determination of passwords, nominating selected terminals) will *itself* be restricted to senior personnel, other than intended users;

(f) a special file may be maintained in the central processor which records every occasion on which access is made by particular terminals and operators to central programs and files; this log will be printed out at regular intervals, e.g. the end of each day, or on request by personnel with appropriate authority.

## Real-Time Systems

In some computer applications a buffer store of input data will be held by the central processor before accessing the master files; in such cases input from remote terminals may be checked by special scanning programs before main processing commences.

However, in 'real-time' systems action at the terminal causes an immediate response in the central processor, whenever the terminal is on-line. Security against unauthorised input and access outlined above is therefore even more important in real-time systems because:

(a) the effect of the input (whether keyed in on the keyboard typewriter or via punch cards, paper tape, etc.) instantaneously updates the files held in the central processor;

(b) edit-checks on the input are likely to be under the control of the terminal operators themselves.

In view of these control problems most real-time systems will incorporate additional controls over the security of the master files, for example by logging the contents of the files 'before look' and 'after look' respectively.

The use of small computers, be they mini- or micro-computers, continues to spread rapidly in industry and commerce. The very significant reductions in the cost of electronic equipment means that there is no longer any economy of scale in using a large computer, and many organisations are decentralising their computer operations or moving away from computer bureaux in order to obtain the advantages of flexibility and local control by using small computers in their own offices.

These small systems present the auditor with three major problem areas:

(a) the small scale of the department in which a mini-computer is installed will almost certainly mean that there is unsatisfactory segregation of duties surrounding the operation of the equipment. The same person may prepare the original data, feed it into the machine, supervise the processing and distribute the output. Sound application controls must therefore be imposed outside the computer system, i.e. in the clerical area, to counter the low level of internal control which results from the lack of segregation within the EDP area;

(b) the lack of standardisation of programming languages used with small computers means that it is difficult to develop interrogation packages;

(c) Most first-time users, buying a prepackaged system, lack the expertise necessary to modify the systems or to adapt their clerical procedures to changes in business requirements. This can lead to control failures and system errors. In a mini-computer environment, therefore, the auditor may experience difficulty in identifying controls and performing compliance tests upon them. The audit approach may be biased more towards substantive testing.

The most practical audit approach in such circumstances is to review the controls surrounding the computer installation and the systems operated on it, and encourage management to provide the best possible level of control that staffing will allow.

The most common audit problems found with mini-computer installations, arising from the features already described, are:

(a) inadequate *validation* procedures, particularly where terminals are in use, thus leading to high error rates during data entry;

(b) unsatisfactory controls over the *authorisation* of sensitive data — such as changes to supplier names and addresses;

(c) lack of procedures for *back-up* of files, or recovery from equipment failure.

Many of these problems can be avoided, of course, if the auditor is involved during the specification of the computer system.


## Use of Microfilm

The following notes provide guidance on the acceptability of microfilm records and indicate certain of the hazards that might arise if internal controls in this area prove to be ineffective.

As a result of the increased cost of storage and the various Acts of Parliament noted below, a number of companies are now turning to the use of microfilm for storing their accounting records.

*Internally and Externally Generated Documents*

There are basically two different categories of documents — *internally* generated documents, e.g. copy sales invoices, goods inwards notes, etc., and those *externally* generated, e.g. purchase invoices. Generally speaking, microfilm copies of internally generated documents are satisfactory evidence for audit purposes — subject, of course, to the adequacy of the controls in force. It is felt, however, that no matter how good the control procedures relating to externally generated documents, the possibility of their being altered does exist and that it would be extremely difficult, if not impossible, to detect an alteration by an examination of a microfilm copy. (There is also the possibility of failure to microfilm information which might, for instance, be printed or written on the back of the document.) Auditors should therefore give serious consideration to insisting that 'third party' documents be retained in their original form, at least until after the audit has been completed.

In any event, before he can even consider accepting microfilm copies of documents for audit purposes, the auditor must satisfy himself as to the internal control over the microfilming process. These controls will need to ensure that the apropriate information is recorded at the correct time and in the correct form. An audit may be required on the microfilm process itself.

## Microfilm controls

These are similar to controls instituted over computer input and processing, and would be expected to include the following additional matters:

(a) A policy should be formally recorded and approved by senior management, setting out the documents which may be destroyed. All such destructions should be properly authorised in accordance with this policy.
(b) It is important for audit purposes that the company should arrange for the microfilming to be done under adequate supervision (for example by the internal audit department or other responsible official independent of the microfilming personnel) and the external auditors should carry out such tests of the above procedures as they consider necessary.
(c) Special registers should be maintained, using batch numbers to record and control the documents microfilmed and destroyed respectively.
(d) Indexing and the retrieval controls should ensure that the company is able to refer quickly and easily to any microfilms of documents.
(e) A complete set of back-up films should be maintained at a different location from that of the originals.

In order that the auditors may have access to the microfilm records, a reader would have to be made constantly available to them during the audit.

## Audit Planning

It is essential that auditors liaise with their clients before a microfilm system is installed, otherwise they may find, too late, that essential records have been destroyed. It is hoped, also, that no records will have been destroyed before the audit report is signed, but should clients so wish, it should only take place after discussion with the auditors, and may necessitate audit visits on a more regular basis.

## Relevant Acts of Parliament

Civil Evidence Act 1972
Stock Exchange Completion of Bargains Act 1976
Companies Act 1948 (Section 436)
Companies Act 1976 (Section 12).

# 21   The SSAP Checklist

*The proliferation of accounting Standards has produced the need for yet another checklist in the bulging audit files. From the point of view of both accountants and auditors (who, under the new auditing Standards, are required to comment on all unwarranted departures from Standards) this checklist has become a necessity. It is equally invaluable for students' use during their examination revision period.*

## SSAP 1 — Accounting for the Results of Associated Companies (Revised April 1982)

1. Does the company:
   (a) have a relationship of partner in a joint venture or consortium with any other company/companies? or
   (b) hold at least 20% of the equity rights of any other company/companies?
   (If 'no' to (a) *and* (b), stop here.)
2. If the answer to (a) *or* (b) above is 'yes', does the investing company exercise influence over the financial and policy decisions of the other company/companies concerned?
3. If the answer to Question 2 is 'no', do the company/group accounts give full particulars of the·names of, and interests in, companies in which the holding is 20% or more of voting rights, but *not* treated as associates?
4. Do the *investing* company's accounts show its share of dividends received, *and* dividends declared by the associate up to the present time?
5. Do we consider the investing company's share of the associate's profits to be material and, if so, do the *group* accounts show the correct amounts of the investing company's share of the associate's profits, retained by the associate?
6. Does investing company's balance sheet show investment in associate at cost less any write-offs?
7. Does group's balance sheet show investment at cost (less write-offs) *plus* share of associate's retained profits?
8. Do the investing group's/company's accounts separately identify (a) group, and (b) associate company reserves, including revaluation reserves?
9. Do the group accounts disclose (a) the investing group's share of any goodwill in the associate's own financial statements, together with (b) the premium paid on the acquisition of interest in the associated company, so far as not written off? ((a) and (b) may be shown as an aggregate.)
10. Have the same criteria been used for acceptance of unaudited accounts of the associate as would apply in the audit of group accounts?
11. If associate's accounts are unaudited, are we satisfied as to their reliability?
12. Do the company/group accounts give full particulars of names of, and interests in, all companies treated as associates?
13. Have we referred to the Standard to check points of detail on:
    (a) extraordinary profits/losses of associate?
    (b) need for more comprehensive disclosure regarding *turnover* and *depreciation* of significant associates?
    (c) accounting adjustments for material unrealised profits?
    (d) accounting dates used?

(e) special circumstances affecting the decision to include/exclude a company as an 'associate'?

(f) restrictions on distribution?

(g) minority interests in the investment in associates?

*Notes:* The definition and interpretation of the term 'associate' left room for confusion and abuse by placing too much emphasis on ownership. A revised definition, and further disclosure details concerning the goodwill of associate companies, was published as part of the revised Standard in April 1982, which further expanded the 'equity' concept of accounting for associates.

## SSAP 2 — Disclosure of Accounting Policies

1. Is there any reason to believe that the company is not operating as a going concern (see separate checklist for criteria in Chapter 10)? (If answer is 'yes' or uncertain, refer matter at once to firm's audit review committee.)

2. Have there been any changes in accounting policy since publication of the last accounts?

3. If answer to previous question is 'yes'
   (a) are reasons for changes stated in the accounts?
   (b) have necessary adjustments in respect of 'prior-year items' been made and disclosed (see SSAP 6)?

4. Have all known and foreseeable losses been provided for?

5. Are all accounting policies stated regarding material items in the following categories:
   basis of consolidation?
   basis of foreign currency translation?
   basis of depreciation?
   basis of valuing stocks and work-in-progress?
   basis of accounting for deferred tax?
   basis of accounting for inflation?
   basis of accounting for research and development expenditure?
   basis of accounting for goodwill arising on acquisitions?

6. Would disclosure of any other accounting policies materially enhance a true and fair view of the company's results and state of affairs, bearing in mind the particular activities of *this* company?

## SSAP 3 — Earnings per Share

1. Are any of the company's equities listed on a recognised stock exchange? (If 'no', stop here.)

2. Is it exempt from disclosure of earnings per share (EPS) because it claims and has been granted exemption under Part III Schedule 2 Companies Act 1967? (If 'yes', stop here.)

3. Are EPS disclosed on the face of the profit and loss account for the current and previous accounting periods?

4. Have any further shares been issued during the year by way of:
   bonus?
   rights?
   full market value issue?

5. Has the appropriate basis of calculation been used in each case?

6. Does the company have in issue securities convertible into ordinary shares at a later date?

7. If answer to previous question is 'yes', have fully diluted EPS been disclosed *in addition to* the information given above?

8. Are the bases of all EPS calculations disclosed by way of a note?

9. Have we referred to the Standard to check points of detail on:
   (a) methods of calculating basic EPS?
   (b) criteria determining requirement to disclose fully diluted EPS?
   (c) adjustment of previous years' figures for the purpose of historical summaries of financial statistics?
   (d) apportionment of EPS over different classes of ordinary shares, if applicable?

## SSAP 4 — Accounting Treatment of Government Grants

1. Does the company qualify for Government grants under the Industry Act 1972 in respect of capital expenditure incurred during the year?
2. Is such a grant reflected in the accounts by either:
   (a) deducting the grant from the cost of the asset? or
   (b) treating the grant as a deferred credit
       (i) portions being credited to the profit and loss account annually;
       (ii) the deferred credit being disclosed in the balance sheet separately from shareholders' funds?
3. If the grant is treated as a deferred credit, are allocations, based on the expected remaining useful life of the asset, transferred annually to profit and loss account?
4. If material, is deferred credit disclosed separately in the balance sheet, but *not* as part of shareholders' funds?

## SSAP 5 — Accounting for VAT

1. Has turnover been shown *net* of VAT on taxable outputs?
2. Has irrecoverable VAT allocable to fixed assets (e.g. company cars), and other items separately disclosed in published accounts, been included in their cost where practicable and material?

## SSAP 6 — Extraordinary Items and Prior Year Adustments

1. Do the accounts include any *material* items which
   (a) derive from events or transactions outside the ordinary activities of the business? and
   (b) are not expected to recur frequently or regularly?
2. Are the nature and size of these disclosed as separate items in the profit and loss account, less any taxation attributable to them, under the heading of 'extraordinary items'?
3. Do the accounts include any 'exceptional' items which, though abnormal in size and incidence, do *not* derive from events or transactions *outside* the ordinary activities of the business?
4. Are the nature and size of (3) above disclosed *before* tax and extraordinary items?
5. Have *unrealised* surpluses, if any, on fixed assets been credited direct to reserves?
6. Has the profit and loss account balance brought forward been adjusted in respect of *material* "prior year" items arising from (a) changes of accounting policy, or (b) the correction of fundamental errors?
7. Have the nature and size of such changes been disclosed?
8. Is the company's determination of whether an item is extraordinary *consistent* (see SSAP 2) with that adopted in previous years, with special reference to:
   (a) disposals of fixed assets, and the differences between written down values and sale proceeds on such disposal?
   (b) discontinuance of a significant part of the business?

(c) sequestration/expropriation/nationalisation of assets?

(d) disposal of shares not acquired for resale (e.g. in associated companies and subsidiaries)?

(e) goodwill/reserves arising on acquisitions?

9. Have extraordinary items correctly been ignored in the calculation of EPS (see SSAP 3)?

## SSAP 8 — The Treatment of Taxation under the Imputation System in the Accounts of Companies

1. Are the following items included in the taxation charge in the profit and loss account and, where material, separately disclosed:

(a) corporation tax charge on income of the year (including transfers to/from deferred taxation account)?

(b) tax attributable to franked investment income (franked investment income being grossed up *pro rata*)?

(c) irrecoverable ACT?

(d) relief for overseas taxation?

(e) total overseas taxation relieved/unrelieved?

2. Are dividends paid and payable shown in the profit and loss account at the amount receivable by shareholders, and the related ACT included in the total corporation tax charge?

3. Has ACT on proposed dividends regarded as recoverable been debited to deferred taxation account?

4. Has provision for ACT on proposed dividends not payable until after the year end been included in current liabilities?

5. In the case of preference shares issued prior to 6 April 1973, has the revised rate of dividend been incorporated in the description of these shares?

## SSAP 9 — Stocks and Work-in-Progress

1. Is stock valued in the accounts at the lower of cost and net realisable value of either:

(a) separate items of stock? or

(b) groups of similar items?

2. Has the value of work-in-progress on long-term contracts been calculated at cost plus attributable profit, less foreseeable losses and progress payments received and receivable?

3. If foreseeable losses exceed cost incurred to date less progress payments recieved and receivable, is the excess shown separately as a provision?

4. Does the valuation of all work in progress and finished goods incorporate a reasonable allocation of attributable overhead expenses, on a basis consistent with that adopted in earlier years, and by other businesses in the same trade?

5. Do the published accounts or notes disclose:

(a) accounting policies used (see SSAP 2) to calculate cost/net realisable value/attributable profit/foreseeable losses?

(b) the *classes* of stock and work-in-progress, indicating the amount of each category classified under headings appropriate to the business?

(c) the value of work-in-progress on long-term contracts at cost, *plus* attributable profits, *less* foreseeable losses?

6. Has compliance with SSAP 9 necessitated a change of accounting policy on valuation of stocks and/or work-in-progress, and, if so:

(a) has the effect of this change been quantified and disclosed in a note to the accounts in order to comply with the Companies Act 1981 and SSAP 2?

(b) have adjustments to the previous year's figures, necessitated by the implementation of SSAP 9, been treated as prior-year adjustments in accordance with SSAP 6?

7. Have we (i) considered, and (ii) reconciled, possible conflict between SSAP 9, on valuation of work-in-progress and long-term contracts, and SSAP 2 with special reference to the accruals and prudence concepts?

## SSAP 10 — Statements of Source and Application of Funds

1. Is turnover of company/group greater than £25,000 p.a.? (If 'no', stop here.)
2. Do the accounts include a statement of source and application of funds for both the current and the corresponding previous period?
3. Are the following items, if applicable, separately disclosed in the statement?
   (a) profit or loss for the period (before tax and extraordinary items, less minority interests)?
   (b) adjustments for profit and loss account items which did not involve a movement of funds during the period?
   (c) funds from other sources, if material?.
   (d) dividends paid during the period?
   (e) acquisitions and disposals of fixed and other non-current assets, and has 'netting-off' been avoided wherever possible?
   (f) funds raised by increasing medium/long-term loans or the issued capital of the company/group?
   (g) funds used in repaying or redeeming medium/long-term loans or issued capital?
   (h) increase/decrease in working capital, subdivided into movements in cash; short-term investments; short-term loans; and its other component elements?
4. Do the page references, and stated scope of the audit examination, in the audit report clearly include the statement of source and application of funds?

## SSAP 12 — Accounting for Depreciation

1. Does the company provide for depreciation of fixed assets having a finite useful life over periods expected to benefit from their use?
2. Is the charge established fairly, exercising sound allocation principles, and based on revalued amounts if the latter are incorporated in the records?
3. Where the estimated asset lives are revised, is the unamortised cost being charged over the revised period?
4. Has any irrecoverable unamortised cost been written off, current charges being based on the remaining cost after the write down of the assets concerned?
5. Has the accounting policy on depreciation changed, and a revised charge established accordingly?
6. If the answer to (5) is 'yes', and the new charge is materially different, do the accounts disclose the effect of the change in accordance with SSAP 6, including the effect on the prior year's figures?
7. If properties are not investment properties (see SSAP 19), has adequate distinction been made between the value of buildings and land respectively, for purposes of determining a fair depreciation charge for the wear and tear of buildings?

## SSAP 13 — Accounting for Research and Development Expenditure

1. Has the company incurred any expenditure on research and development?
   (If 'no', stop here.)

2. Was the expenditure incurred in locating and exploiting mineral deposits?
   (If 'yes', stop here, since such expenditure is exempt from SSAP 13 treatment.)
3. Has the company incurred any expenditure on market research?
   (If 'yes', it should be written off in year incurred unless it satisfies the deferral criteria for development expenditure.)
4. Does any of the expenditure form the subject of a firm contract recoverable from third parties?
   (If 'yes', this should be carried forward as work-in-progress in the balance sheet, until recovered.)
5. Has the company incurred any expenditure on *pure* or *applied* research?
   (If 'yes', this should be written off against revenues for the year).
6. Has the company incurred development expenditure which satisfies the criteria set out in Paragraph 12 of the Standard?
   (If 'yes', it may be carried forward to future accounting periods only so far as its recoverability can reasonably be assured.)
7. Does the company apply its policy of deferring R&D expenditure consistently?
8. Has all recoverable development expenditure been written off so that amounts carried forward represent the estimated recoverable amount in the light of a judgement of all surrounding evidence and circumstances?
9. Have we checked that R&D expenditure once written off has not been reinstated?
10. Has depreciation been charged against any R&D carried forward?
    (If 'yes', it should be adequately disclosed in accordance with SSAP 12, if material.)
11. Do disclosures in the accounts adequately explain movements in sums carried forward, the basis adopted, and the company's accounting policy with respect to R&D expenditure?
12. Does accounting treatment affect sums available for dividend under Sections 39 and 42 of the Companies Act 1980?

## SSAP 14 — Consolidated Financial Statements

1. Can it be established that a group exists as defined in the Companies Act 1948?
   (If 'yes', the holding company should prepare group accounts in the form of a single set of consolidated financial statements dealing with the holding company and its subsidiaries.)
2. If subsidiaries are excluded, have conditions set out in Section 150 (2) (a) & (b), Companies Act 1948, been satisfied? (See Paragraphs 19–28 of the Standard.)
3. Are uniform accounting policies observed throughout the group?
   (If 'no', appropriate adjustments should be made to bring accounts of individual subsidiaries into line with group accounting policy. Where subsidiaries, due to impracticality, do not follow uniform policies, accounts should indicate the different policies used, amounts of assets and liabilities involved, the effect of such policies, and the reason for their adoption.)
4. Are the accounts of the subsidiaries co-terminous with the group's accounting reference date?
   (If 'no', Department of Trade approval is required. After receipt of D.o.T. approval, accounts may require adjustment for abnormal transactions falling between respective accounting dates. In respect of each subsidiary with a different accounting date, the name, accounting date, reason for different date, and the period covered by the accounts, must be clearly disclosed.)
5. Has there been a change in the composition of the group during the period under review?
   (If 'yes', the effective date of acquisition/disposal will be the earlier of the date on which consideration passes or on which offer is declared unconditional.)
6. Have there been significant additions to the companies within the group?
   (If 'yes', the consolidated financial statements should disclose the effect of such additions on the consolidated profit and loss accounts.)

105

7. Has purchase consideration been allocated over the underlying assets of subsidiaries on the basis of a fair valuation?
   (If 'no', such allocation must be reflected in the consolidated accounts.)
8. Has a material disposal taken place within the accounting period?
   (If 'yes', the consolidated profit and loss account should include profits of subsidiaries up to the date of disposal, and any gain/loss computed should be reflected as an extraordinary item.)
9. Do the accounts disclose minority interests separately from shareholders' funds?
   (Debit balances in relation to minorities should be shown as such only if the loss can be met by the minority.)
10. Does the consolidated profit and loss account disclose the minority share of profits including sums relating to extraordinary items?
11. Do the accounts disclose the name, proportion of nominal value of shares held, and nature of the business, for each particular class of subsidiary within the group?

## SSAP 15 — Accounting for Deferred Taxation

1. Has deferred taxation been accounted for on all short-term timing differences?
   (Unless the company can satisfy the criteria in Paragraph 3 of the Standard, deferred taxation should be provided for in respect of material originating timing differences — i.e. in respect of capital allowances, stock relief, revaluation surpluses, and roll-over relief.)
2. Is the company a going concern?
3. If the answer to (2) is 'yes', can it be foreseen on reasonable evidence that the timing differences will not reverse for at least three years, and that there is no present indication that after this period the liability is likely to crystallise?
   (If 'yes', deferred taxation need not be provided.)
4. Have we reviewed the situation covered by the previous two questions in the course of each of the years audited, with due regard to the company's pattern of capital expenditure, stock levels, and cash flow/profit forecasts?
   (The need for a partial amount of deferred tax provision in respect of originating timing differences should be considered.)
5. Is there a debit balance on deferred taxation account?
   (If 'yes', it should be written off unless recoverability is reasonably certain.)
6. Has the company incurred trading losses?
   (If 'yes', these should not normally be reflected in the deferred taxation account. If, exceptionally, they are so reflected, the amounts should be limited to the notional tax attributable to the loss.)
7. Does the profit and loss account adequately disclose (a) deferred taxation as a separate component of the total tax charge; and (b) the amounts attributable to extraordinary items?
8. Do the notes to the balance sheet disclose (a) deferred taxation separately from shareholders' funds; (b) the basis of the deferred taxation provision selected as an accounting policy; (c) movements on the deferred taxation account; and (d) the potential and actual amounts of deferred taxation attributable to each particular category of timing difference?

## SSAP 16 — Current Cost Accounting

In view of the complexity of SSAP 16 provisions, students may find the flow diagrams in Figures 2–6 more useful than an SSAP checklist. These diagrams have been devised by Deloitte, Haskins and Sells, whose kind permission to reproduce them is duly acknowledged.

106

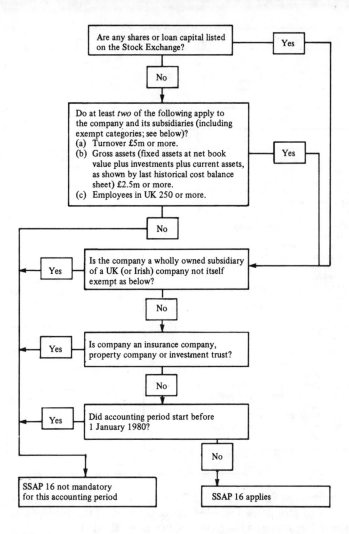

**Figure 2** Scope of SSAP 16. Note: SSAP 16 is not intended to apply to charities, building societies, trade unions, pension funds or unit trusts.

### SSAP 17 — Accounting for Post-Balance Sheet Events

*Definition*: Post-balance sheet events are those events, both favourable and unfavourable, which occur between the balance sheet date and the date on which the financial statements are approved by the board of directors.

1. Have the financial statements been prepared on the basis of conditions existing at the balance sheet date?
   2. Have all material post balance sheet events which:

  (a) are adjusting events, providing additional evidence of conditions existing at the balance sheet date; or

  (b) indicate that application of the going concern concept to the whole or a material part of the company is not appropriate,

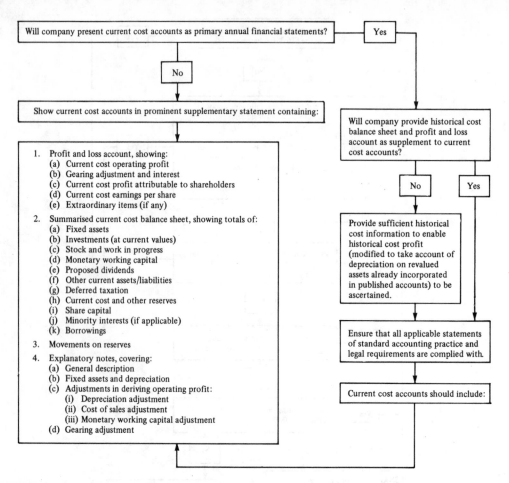

**Figure 3** Requirements of SSAP 16. Note: This applies to individual companies if they do not have subsidiaries, or to groups as a whole (taking account of the exemptions specified in SSAP 16). Reference should be made to the guidance notes no SSAP 16, published by the Accounting Standards Committee, for the comprehensive requirements in the case of groups of companies and certain special cases.

resulted in changes being made in the amounts included in the financial statements?

3. Have all any material post balance sheet events which should be disclosed by way of note in the financial statements been so shown? Note: Such events must be either:

(a) non-adjusting events of such materiality that non-disclosure would affect the ability of the user of the financial statements to reach a proper understanding of the financial position; or

(b) the reversal or maturity after the year end of an transaction entered into before the year end, the substance of which was primarily to alter the appearance of the company's balance sheet ('window-dressing').

4. If disclosure is made by way of note, have the following been stated:

108

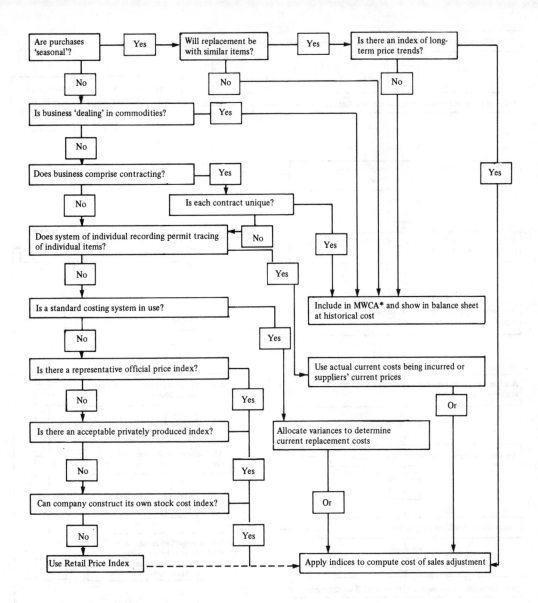

**Figure 4** Method of calculation for stock, work-in-progress, different sections of (COSA). Note: This can be applied to the entire stock and work-in-progress, different sections of the business, groups of similar items, individual materials, or for different cost elements, as appropriate for the type of business. *see Figure 6.

(a) the nature of the event; and
(b) an estimate of the financial effect, or a statement that it is not practicable to make such an estimate?

5. Has any estimate of the financial effect been disclosed before taking account of taxation, and the taxation implications explained where necessary?

6. Do the financial statements disclose the date on which they were approved by the directors?

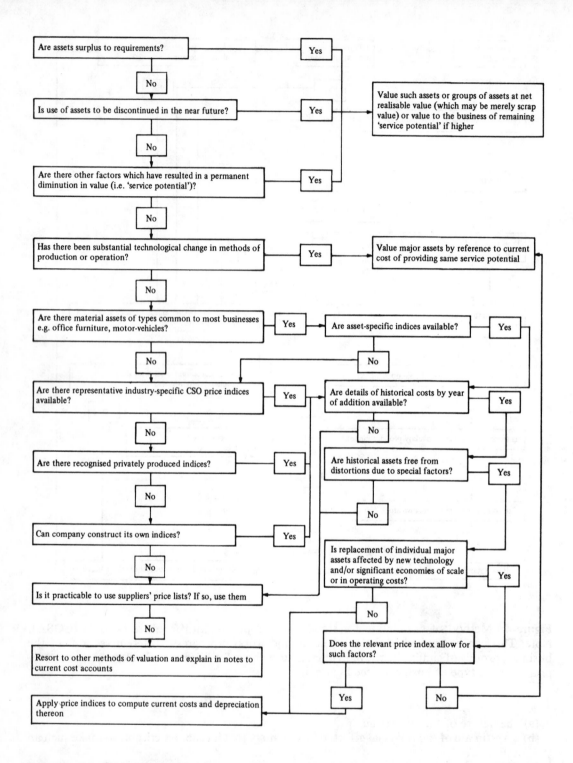

**Figure 5** Method of calculation for plant and machinery. Note: This can be applied to blocks of similar assets, though the grouping together of similar assets will depend on the availability of indices and other circumstances set out above.

110

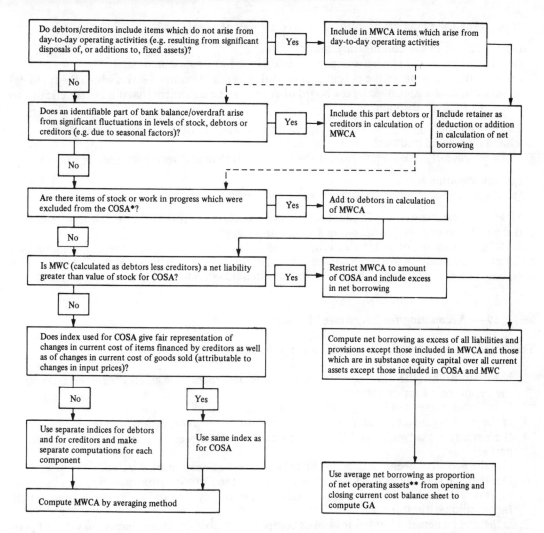

**Figure 6** Method of calculation of monetary working capital adjustment (MWCA) and gearing adjustment (GA). *see Figure 5. **fixed assets, stocks and MWC.

## SSAP 18 — Accounting for Contingencies

*Definition*: Contingency is a condition which exists at the balance sheet date where the outcome will be confirmed only on the occurrence or non-occurrence of one or more uncertain future events.

1. Have all material contingent losses been accrued in the financial statements where

   (a) it is probable that a future event will confirm the loss; and
   (b) the loss can be estimated with reasonable accuracy at the date on which the financial statements are approved by the board?

2. Have material contingent losses (which are not accrued) been disclosed in the financial statements?

If so, is the following information disclosed by way of notes:

(a) the nature of the contingency, and
(b) the uncertainties which are expected to affect the ultimate outcome, and
(c) a prudent estimate of the potential financial effect made at the date on which the financial statements are approved by the board of directors or a statement that it is not practicable to make such an estimate?

3. Have all contingent gains been excluded from accruals in the financial statements, and only disclosed if material and likely to be realised?

4 .In the case of a contingent loss, is the potential financial effect disclosed net of:

(a) any amounts accrued;
(b) the amounts of any components where the possibility of loss is remote?

5. Has any estimate of the financial effect been disclosed before taking account of taxation, and the taxation implications explained where necessary?

6. Where the nature of and the uncertainties affecting a contingency in respect of an individual transaction are common to a large number of transactions, has the estimate of the financial effect been based on the group of transactions without individually disclosing each contingency?


## SSAP 19 — Accounting for Investment Properties

This Standard deals with assets excluded from the scope of SSAP 12.

1. Have we checked the wording of the Standard to ensure that the assets concerned fall within the definition of 'investment property'?
2. Is the property owned by a charity? (If 'yes', stop here.)
3. Is the property held on lease, and, if so, is the unexpired term 20 years or less?
4. If answer to (3) is 'yes', has depreciation under SSAP 12 been provided over the remaining period?
5. Has the property been included in the balance sheet at open market value?
6. Do financial statements disclose names of valuers, their professional qualifications, and the bases of valuation used by them? (If a valuer is an employee or officer of the company, that fact should be disclosed.)
7. Is the client a pension fund or insurance company in whose accounts changes in value of properties are dealt with in the relevant fund accounts? (If 'yes', Questions 8 and 9 below do not apply.)
8. Have valuation changes been disclosed as a movement on the investment revaluation reserve?
9. If movement arising from (7) above produces a deficit, has the deficit been correctly charged to profit and loss account? (This does not necessarily apply to investment trusts, or property unit trusts.)
10. Do the financial statements prominently display the carrying value of investment properties and the investment revaluation reserve?